art
and
reproduction

art
and
reproduction

GRAPHIC REPRODUCTION TECHNIQUES

RAYMOND A. BALLINGER

VNR **VAN NOSTRAND REINHOLD COMPANY**
New York Cincinnati Toronto London Melbourne

Also by Raymond A. Ballinger:
Layout and Graphic Design
Lettering Art in Modern Use
Sign, Symbol and Form (with
Louise Bowen Ballinger)

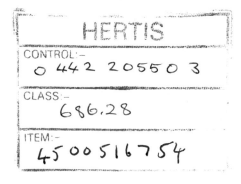
Library of Congress Catalog Card Number 76-5070
ISBN 0-442-20550-3

Printed in Italy by Istituto Italiano d'Arti Grafiche - Bergamo

Published in 1977 by Van Nostrand Reinhold Company
A Division of Litton Educational Publishing, Inc.
450 West 33rd Street
New York, N.Y. 10001

Van Nostrand Reinhold Limited
1410 Birchmount Road
Scarborough, Ontario M1P 2E7, Canada

Van Nostrand Reinhold Australia Pty. Ltd.
17 Queen Street
Mitcham, Victoria 3132, Australia

Van Nostrand Reinhold Company Ltd.
Molly Millars Lane
Wokingham, Berkshire, England

16 15 14 13 12 11 10 9 8 7 6 5 4 3 2 1

Library of Congress Cataloging in Publication Data

Ballinger, Raymond A 1907–
   Art and reproduction.

   Bibliography: p.
   Includes Index.
   1. Printing, Practical. I. Title
Z244.B2   686.2'24   76-5070
ISBN 0-442-20550-3

CONTENTS

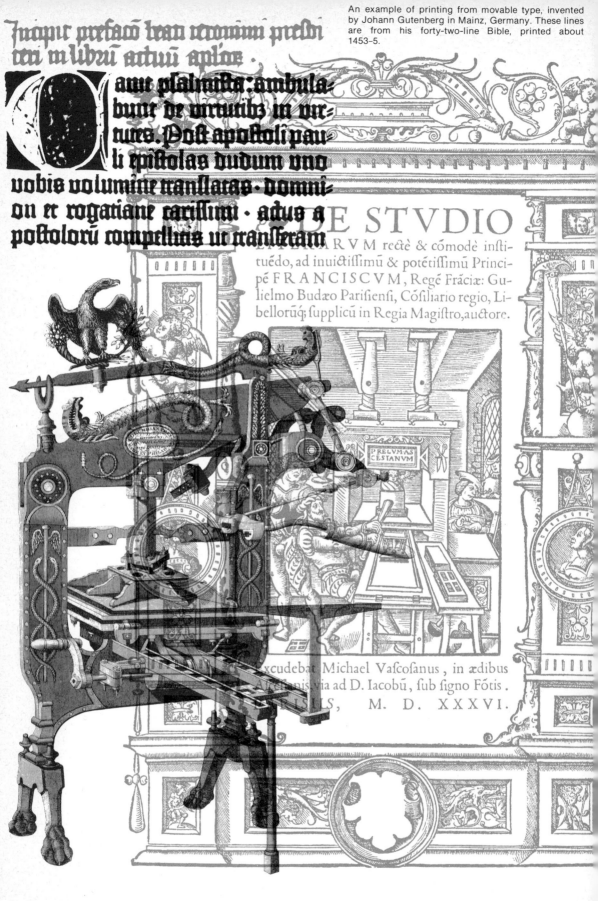

An example of printing from movable type, invented by Johann Gutenberg in Mainz, Germany. These lines are from his forty-two-line Bible, printed about 1453–5.

An engraving of a Columbian printing press made in Philadelphia in 1813.

A title page by Michel Vascosan, Paris, 1536. The central illustration shows an early printing press. From *200 Decorative Title Pages*, edited by Alexander Nesbitt, Dover Publications, Inc., 1964.

FOREWORD

Throughout the history of the arts it is evident that artists have been intensely interested in and excited about their materials and techniques. The properties of pigments, wall surfaces, canvases, papers, stones, and metals—whatever was worked with or upon—were of great concern in facilitating their talents and, hopefully, preserving their achievements. Treatises and books on the subject have been prominent in the libraries of artists, and studies by artists of the techniques of others have contributed greatly to our knowledge of the arts. Artists have traditionally been concerned with one-of-a-kind results; and printmakers, with relatively few copies of woodcuts, etchings, engravings, or lithographs. In recent times many of these earlier productions have been reproduced in vast numbers by contemporary methods, often with exceptional quality. Many artists and craftspeople have made great efforts to increase the volume of production and thus have brought about such inventions as typesetting, printing presses, and reproduction plates.

Outstanding graphic artists today are equally concerned with the techniques of their work, not only on the easel and drawing board but in relation to the materials of production and contemporary methods of reproduction. Fundamental to a good design education, of course, is training in all of the basic arts—drawing, composition, color, techniques and materials (including such fundamentals as lettering, perspective, and anatomy), history of the arts, and on a more advanced level instruction and experimentation in such processes as silk screen, etching and engraving, lithography, and photography. With such an enriching background the professional graphic artist is able to understand the challenges of preparing art and design that will be reproduced in great volume.

One of the most tantalizing problems in graphic-arts education has been the usual lack of interest on the part of students—and too often on the part of their instructors—in the exciting possibilities of reproduction and printing methods. There is much comment in the professional field about young designers who wish to be stars but who are concerned little with the really exciting aspects of design preparation, production, and printing, which can make their work vital, valuable, and effective and which should result in its finest aesthetic fulfillment.

We live in a mechanized world—often a computerized world—and the graphic artist is caught up in this. It is interesting that in many areas of arts and crafts there is a tendency to return to a craftlike approach and move away from the more impersonal implications of machine methods. Beginning with or returning to the craft approach in calligraphy, typesetting, or printmaking by hand may be recommended as a very important educational, psychological, and aesthetic experience. Today's graphic artist will not be called upon to operate a printing press producing hundreds of copies per hour or, on the other hand, to operate an old handpress. *Fortune* magazine has stated this concept neatly in an article entitled "Printing": "Printing is an old, diffuse and complex industry, with roots still in the ancient handicrafts, despite great modern presses and mechanical speeds."

This book is not a how-to-do-it publication. It is intended to be an inspirational book to help young designers to be *total* designers through their interest in design, preparatory, and reproduction processes and in the contemporary materials at their command.

This mammoth machine is typical of multiple-color printing presses in use today that make possible fast, long runs. Operators of such machinery are highly paid, and much of the process is controlled automatically. It is important for designers to have some knowledge of the techniques and equipment used to prepare and print their designs so that they can use their creative talents in the best manner. The press shown here is from the Stern Majestic Press plant in Philadelphia. The photograph is courtesy of American-Standard, Inc., New York.

Pencil line drawing by the author.

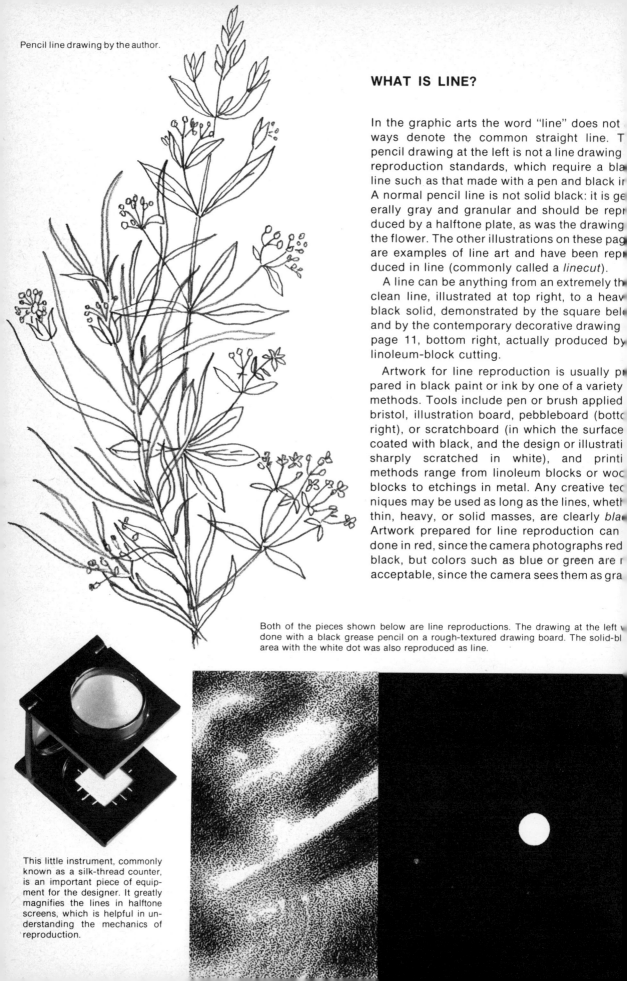

WHAT IS LINE?

In the graphic arts the word "line" does not
ways denote the common straight line. T
pencil drawing at the left is not a line drawing
reproduction standards, which require a bla
line such as that made with a pen and black in
A normal pencil line is not solid black: it is ge
erally gray and granular and should be repr
duced by a halftone plate, as was the drawing
the flower. The other illustrations on these pag
are examples of line art and have been repr
duced in line (commonly called a *linecut*).

A line can be anything from an extremely th
clean line, illustrated at top right, to a heav
black solid, demonstrated by the square bel
and by the contemporary decorative drawing
page 11, bottom right, actually produced by
linoleum-block cutting.

Artwork for line reproduction is usually pr
pared in black paint or ink by one of a variety
methods. Tools include pen or brush applied
bristol, illustration board, pebbleboard (botto
right), or scratchboard (in which the surface
coated with black, and the design or illustrati
sharply scratched in white), and printi
methods range from linoleum blocks or woc
blocks to etchings in metal. Any creative tec
niques may be used as long as the lines, whetr
thin, heavy, or solid masses, are clearly *bla*
Artwork prepared for line reproduction can
done in red, since the camera photographs red
black, but colors such as blue or green are r
acceptable, since the camera sees them as gra

Both of the pieces shown below are line reproductions. The drawing at the left v
done with a black grease pencil on a rough-textured drawing board. The solid-bl
area with the white dot was also reproduced as line.

This little instrument, commonly
known as a silk-thread counter,
is an important piece of equipment for the designer. It greatly
magnifies the lines in halftone
screens, which is helpful in un-
derstanding the mechanics of
reproduction.

A decorative and delicate drawing,
admirably suited to line reproduction.

vigorous block print from a
stmas card by Morris Berd is
emporary in spirit and looks
nificent as line reproduction.

The line illustrations on these pages were repro
duced from old books and encyclopedias. They
are remarkable for the success achieved using
line only to create a tonal effect. Before the in
vention of the camera and the halftone screen
artists used many techniques, all in line, to create
effects of shadow, depth, and dimension. These
techniques are still valid and are used advantage
ously by contemporary designers. Line repro
duction is economical and particularly useful fo
printing on poorer grades of paper such as news
print and kraft.

Trompe l'oeil is the French term for the visua
deception involved here, which is even more ap
parent in the three illustrations on the following
pages. The abstract design at the top of page 1
is done in black and white alone, but if you star
at it a moment, your eye will be fooled into seein
areas of gray. The charming illustration at th
bottom of the page creates a tantalizing sense c
jumpy motion simply by duplicating the lines of
basic drawing. On page 15 a contemporary draw
ing, prepared in line only but reproduced in tw
colors, creates a strong optical illusion of curve
and depth.

Typical of engraved plates and illustrations of the perio
this section of an elaborate print from the early eighteen
century shows the methods employed to create depth ar
form, light and shade with thick and thin lines and cris
crossing. As printed here it is strictly a line reproduction.

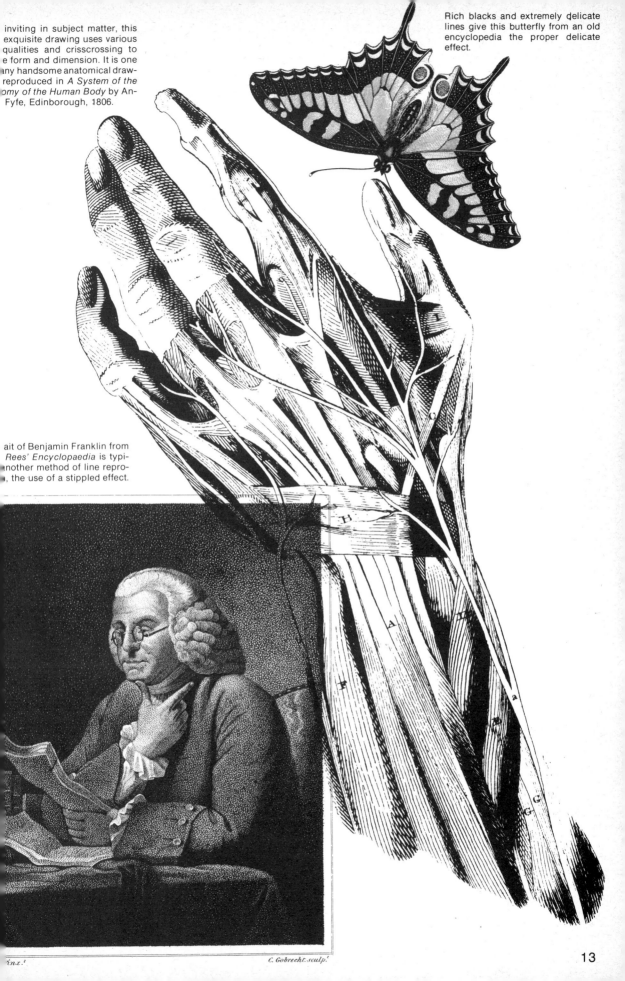

inviting in subject matter, this exquisite drawing uses various qualities and crisscrossing to ⸺e form and dimension. It is one ⸺any handsome anatomical draw-⸺reproduced in *A System of the* ⸺omy of the Human Body by An-⸺Fyfe, Edinborough, 1806.

Rich blacks and extremely delicate lines give this butterfly from an old encyclopedia the proper delicate effect.

⸺ait of Benjamin Franklin from *Rees' Encyclopaedia* is typi-⸺nother method of line repro-⸺, the use of a stippled effect.

⸺nx.ᵗ

C. Gobrecht. sculp.ᵗ

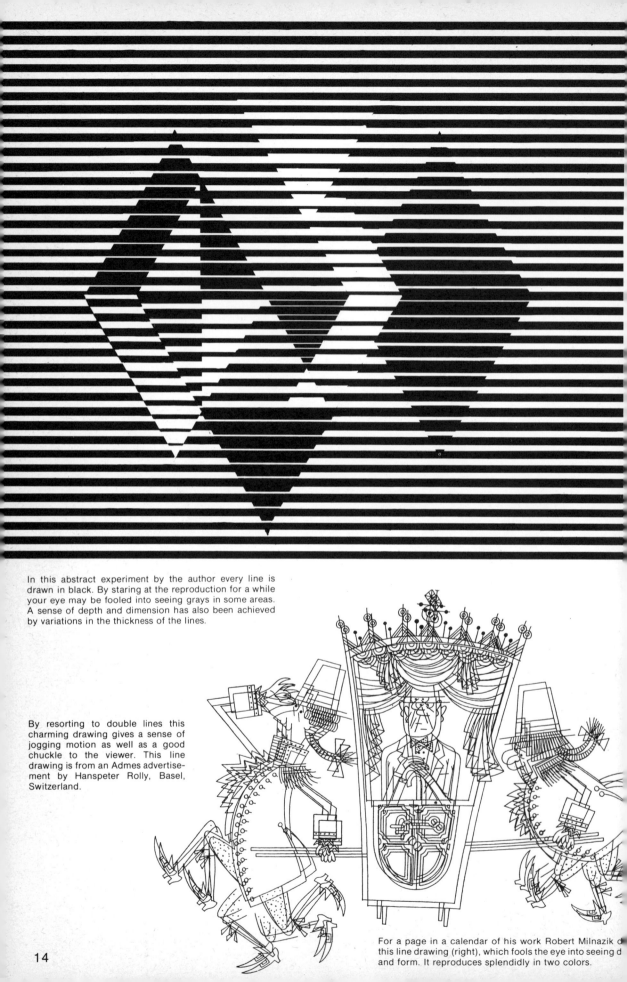

In this abstract experiment by the author every line is drawn in black. By staring at the reproduction for a while your eye may be fooled into seeing grays in some areas. A sense of depth and dimension has also been achieved by variations in the thickness of the lines.

By resorting to double lines this charming drawing gives a sense of jogging motion as well as a good chuckle to the viewer. This line drawing is from an Admes advertisement by Hanspeter Rolly, Basel, Switzerland.

For a page in a calendar of his work Robert Milnazik d this line drawing (right), which fools the eye into seeing d and form. It reproduces splendidly in two colors.

Taking advantage of line techniques and m
ipulating them to get unusual results are a c
stant and interesting design challenge.
signers often realize that limited budgets
necessary but that their final results must
unusual and distinctive. The decorative pi
below came from a black-and-white print m
from an old woodcut used for fabric printing
was reproduced with a 20% screen of black
to achieve the gray effect. It creates an appro
ate letterhead for the wife of the author, who i
artist and an art teacher. Spontaneous c
graphy in line, reproduced at the right, makes
exceptionally attractive menu cover. In
original reproduction the bold dots were in br
colors.

Facing page:

Menu cover for Pan American Airways, Inc., designed by Ivan Chermayeff of Chermayeff and Geism
Associates, New York.

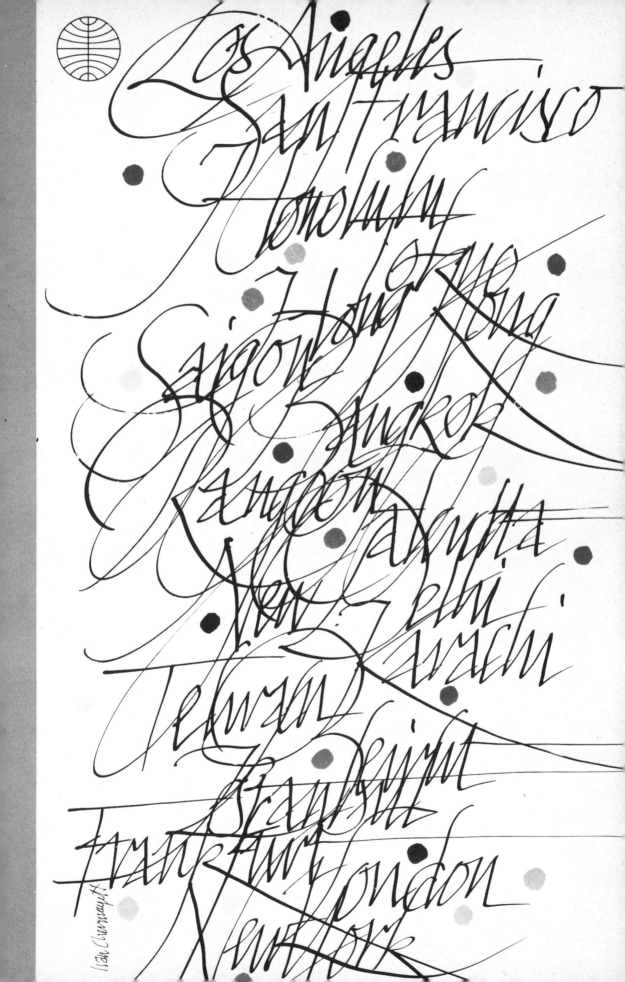

This inquisitive fellow is the Greek owl of wisdom. Originally about 1½" high and in black line, he was enlarged greatly and printed in negative with a solid-color background. This is still a line reproduction, demonstrating that line art may be greatly enlarged—or reduced. On the opposite page the owl was reproduced in many ways to show the versatility of line art.

Reproduced from Ernst Lehner, *Symbols, Signs & Signets*, Dover Publications, Inc.

sitive black line.

2. 50% of black, flopped.

3. Positive blue line.

egative line, black.

5. Negative line, color.

6. Negative line, blue and black.

egative line, 50% of black.

8. Positive black line on color.

9. Negative line, 50% of color.

eduction, white line on blue.

In addition to enlargement or reduction line art challenges the designer in many other imaginative ways. Some of these uses are suggested here, but there can be many variations on the theme of line.

11. Overprinting, color on black.

Reproduction in line was requisite before the invention of photographic screens and related techniques. Before moving on to discuss halftone screens and reproduction, it would be worthwhile to exhibit the reverse of this procedure. For artistic and economic reasons a photograhic negative is sometimes printed in such a manner that it in effect becomes line art and can be reproduced as line. This is usually called *conversion*, and an interesting example of the technique is reproduced here.

Client: Inspiration Consolidated Copper Company, New York, Annual Report
Designer: Jack Derman/Lind Brothers, New York.
Photographer: Norman's Studio, Globe, Arizona.

Overlay and benday screens have long been used as a means of creating tonal effects in line art. The greatest use of this technique is probably for newspaper reproduction and lower-cost advertising material. Intelligently used, it may simulate the visual effects of the halftone screen, but it is still line art and line reproduction. Obviously, these screens are far less expensive than halftone screens.

Because overlay screens are available in a great variety of textures and patterns, they are often advantageously used for decorative as well as tonal value. The illustration on this page is one of several that appear in a series of educational books. The basic illustration is in black line with a light overlay screen. An acetate overlay was prepared using other screen textures and patterns and carefully registered with the first drawing. This was also reproduced in line but in color, resulting in an interesting and lively effect, attractive to young people and achieved at moderate cost.

The decorative border gives some idea of the variety of screens available.

Illustration by Jack Weaver for *Becoming: A Course In Human Relations*, J. B. Lippincott Company, Philadelphia and New York. Design by Sulpizio Studios.

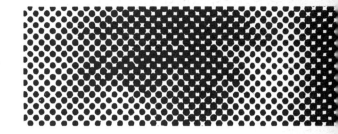

HALFTONES

Trompe l'oeil, which applies to some line art, expresses the very essence of halftone reproduction and four-color printing processes. Remembering that it means "visual deception," this is exactly what happens in printing from a halftone plate and, as you will see on page 32, to an even greater extent in printing from four-color plates.

To explain this phenomenon in the simplest terms, consider a simple photograph or a piece of artwork—for instance, a wash drawing. In both cases think of them as black-and-white originals—not color. In studying these pieces you will note that the values probably range from white or very light gray to intense black; the tones sweep softly from light to dark and from dark to light. Engravers and printers call this a *continuous-tone print*, or continuous-tone artwork. Copies can be made from the original negative of the photograph, but neither of the pieces can be printed in great quantities in a magazine or book. To do this, both the photograph and the artwork must be processed to make a printing plate, in this case a *halftone plate*.

Placing the original photograph or artwork before a special kind of camera, an engraver photographs it through a special screen inscribed with a crisscross of numerous fine lines (often 110) per square inch. This screen causes the image of the original photograph or artwork (often called *copy*) to be broken down on a negative into dots of varying sizes. When the image of this negative is transferred to a printing plate, the dots are transferred, carrying the ink that makes a facsimile impression on the printing surface of the paper as it is fed through the press.

When the printed surface is observed under magnification, the "continuous tone" no longer exists, but the naked eye alone can hardly see the dots created for the printing plate. Therein exists the trompe l'oeil: the platemaking and printing processes have fooled the eye.

For various reasons the engraver may change the number of lines per square inch on the screen, thus changing the size of the dots. For instance, because of the generally poorer quality of newsprint a coarser screen with fewer lines to the square inch (often 65) is generally used. The photograph on page 22 was divided into four areas, each with a different screen, so that the varying effects of the printed images may be observed.

In order to create unusual and interesting visual effects, artists and designers often instruct an engraver or printer to use screens with more or fewer lines to the square inch or to exaggerate the size or character of the dots. This is one of many instances in which a knowledge of printing techniques is important to the artist. Effects of this kind can only be accomplished technically. An example of an extremely exaggerated screen is shown above.

photograph of a tower in Seattle is reproduced
divided halftones to show the effects of four
nt screens. Top left, 100-line screen; top right,
e screen; bottom left, 133-line screen; bottom
110-line screen. Photograph by the author.

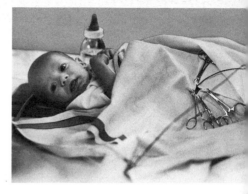

The original proportions of the photograph of the bab[...]

The screens and plates used for halftone reproduction are produced by rigid photographic and mechanical techniques. Their artistic and optical effects, however, are subject to the needs of the project and the ingenuity of the designer in solving problems. The illustration on the opposite page is from an annual report of a children's hospital in which it was desired to convey a sense of technical knowledge and equipment as they relate to the wellbeing of infants and children. Each illustration in the report shows a young patient in the background in a high-key halftone, with a rich, full halftone in the foreground showing medical or surgical equipment. The subjects were two different photographs, each retouched and overlaid so that they related properly to each other. The development of this overlapping technique involved an interesting procedure that required an expert retouching artist competent with an airbrush. The reproductions at the right give some idea as to how the final effect was produced.

The Children's Hospital of Philadelphia, Annual Report, 1971. Director of Information, Mary C. Hope. Design by the author. Photographs by Ed Eckstein.

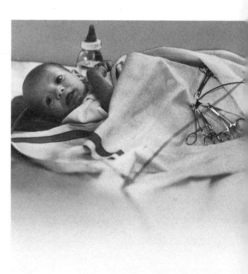

An airbrushed acetate overlay was used to extend the depth of the photograph.

The photograph of the equipment was prepared as a[...] houette, and the background was airbrushed so th[...] overprinted the photograph of the baby.

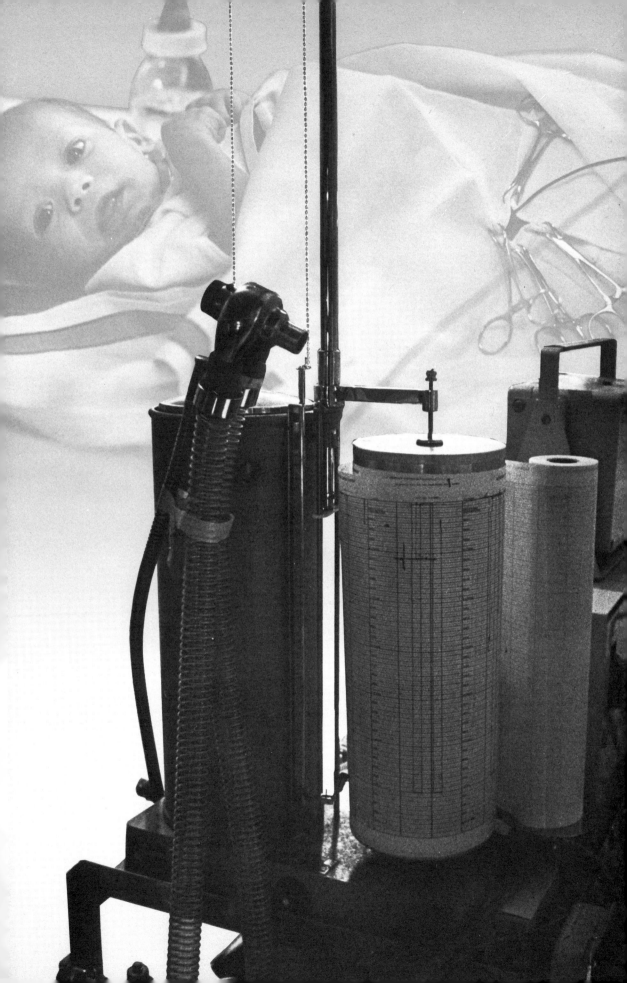

These pages represent a reversal of the basic platemaking technique. The photograph on this page was originally a continuous-tone print, and it was reproduced as a typical halftone. Good designers, however, are aware that they have several options with continuous-tone photographs, particularly if the print has good contrast. *Line conversion* is one of these technical options, shown in the reproductions on the following page. Line conversion is simply a conversion from continuous tone to solid black and white. In the exposure of the line negative white areas record first, then the various gray values record as solid black; the final effect is black and white only with no in-between values.

A variety of effects can be produced relatively inexpensively by line conversion. The results become more interesting by printing on colored papers. The line art itself can be printed in color or on colored paper. And it can also be printed in black over a second color of ink. Imagination is the key to successful use of this technique.

The illustrations on these pages, shown by courte
Kimberly-Clark Corporation, are from a most inforr
publication entitled *Photomechanical Techniques.*

An infinite variety of photomechanical screens may be utilized by the designer together with photoengravers and printers, who can give advice on availability and technical matters. The use of a fine halftone properly related to the paper on which it is printed will most often be practical, but there may be instances when special screen effects are desirable.

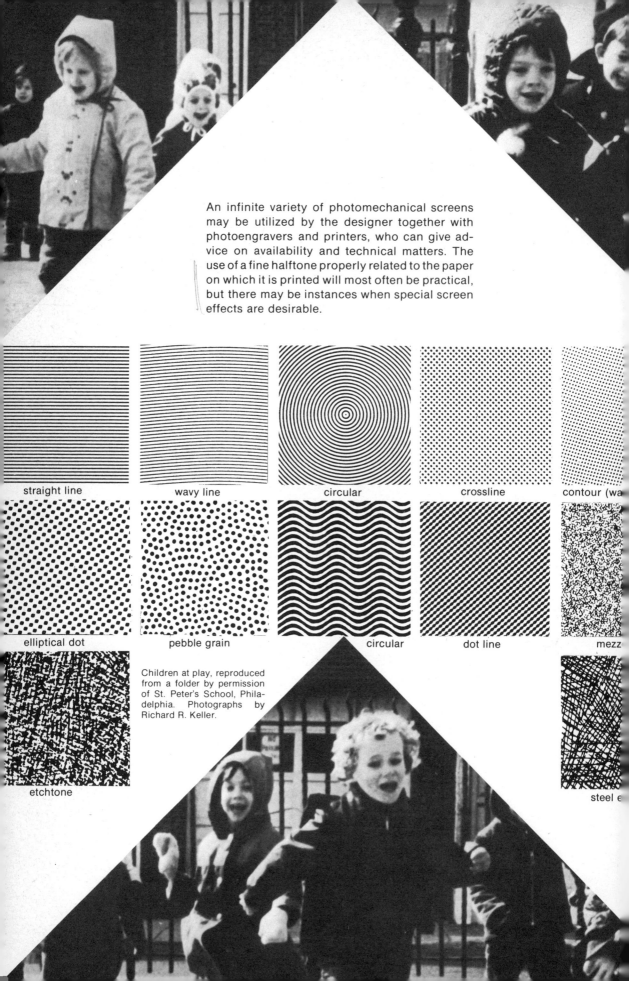

straight line

wavy line

circular

crossline

contour (wa

elliptical dot

pebble grain

circular

dot line

mezz

etchtone

Children at play, reproduced from a folder by permission of St. Peter's School, Philadelphia. Photographs by Richard R. Keller.

steel e

One of a series of mailing pieces entitled *Tools of the Trade*, reproduced by courtesy of Alling and Cory, Rochester, N.Y. The enlarged half-tone screen is essentially a huge line reproduction on a bright Curtis Delmarva Cover paper. Designed by Evans, Garber, Ligas & Page.

In many reproductions the halftone screen is hardly discernible to the naked eye. In this mailing piece the screen was deliberately enlarged to create an exciting optical effect. The actual size of the piece is shown beside the small reproduction. Even at this reduction the screen pattern is very evident.

tools of the trade

22"

18"

Contact print.

The illustrations on these pages show standard procedures that are often used to enhance half-tone reproductions. At the left is a typical reproduction of a photographic contact print. The illustration below shows an enlargement printed in a 110-line screen.

Enlargement reproduced in 110-line screen.

same photograph has been printed in the *duotone* technique. "Duo" s to the use of a second color. The nd color is often very light or soft der to enhance the richness of the oduction. Offset printers try to eve more depth and richness in one reproduction—to create the ession of gravure printing, which recognize to be excellent but costly. *Double-dot* printing helps hieve a richer effect. Double-dot is ntially the use of two screens, one hich prints black, and the other a nd color, usually a gray.

Duotone—black and one color.

us types of screen applications to one reproduction are shown on 28. In this reproduction a mezzo- as used on the black halftone, and s printed over a solid color. It is rtant to remember that halftone oductions do not always have to be hite paper. Imagination may sug- the use of colored papers, but must be taken that the paper will pt the halftone and that readability ot be impaired.

Mezzotint over solid color.

FOUR-COLOR PRINTING

The progression from line reproduction to halftone reproduction to color reproduction reflects exactly the historic progress made in the development of printing. A line or halftone plate is often printed in color, thus extending visual interest and the possibility of more creative effects. Line and halftone plates may also be printed on any of today's galaxy of colored papers, broadening even more the horizon of creativity.

Four-color printing (or four-color process), as well as two- and three-color printing, are basically achieved with halftone plates. It is still surprising to realize that so-called full-color printing is usually the result of four plates, each printing a single color of ink (called *process colors*): red, yellow, blue, and black. If more accuracy or subtlety of color is required, as in printing reproductions of outstanding paintings, additional plates may be used with additional colors of ink. In most full-color printing, however, four plates and four colors are standard.

The principle of trompe l'oeil is very evident in four-color printing, for the dots on the plates not only carry the value relationships but their sizes and positions as they relate to each other in supplying ink to the paper also signal the colors to the eye. Just as a mixture of yellow and red paint creates orange, so the size and position of a yellow dot in relation to a red dot produce an optical effect of orange. Just as a painter may use more or less yellow or red and perhaps small amounts of other colors to change the hue or intensity of the orange, so, too, the four halftone plates, properly made and adjusted, create similar optical effects—fooling the eye into seeing a single color rather than a carefully organized combination of colors.

How is this delicate visual deception accomplished? One of the basic terms in printing four-color work is *color separation*. For a full-color original, whether it is a transparency or reflective art (a photograph or other artwork), to be reproduced in four colors, it must be photographed by the engraver's camera in such a way that four negatives are made—one for each color to be printed. The photographic process of color separation is accomplished by the use of filters that prevent the camera from seeing certain colors during one exposure and other colors during other exposures.

Making four-color plates is a delicate process requiring extremely accurate *register*, the close alignment of plates so that they print together. Making these plates is a precise, technical, time-consuming, and expensive matter. It is for this reason that low-budget assignments cannot be produced by the four-color process. The designer may have to rely on imaginative uses of color that involve fewer plates and less preparation. In such situations the available array of colored printing papers may come in handy.

When full-color printing is indicated, the separations made, the plates applied to the presses, and the color proofs made, corrected, and/or approved, the presses are ready to roll. The press may print one or more colors at a time, or a huge four-color press may print all the colors at the same time. In any event this is a breathtaking moment—to see sheets or rolls of white paper move through presses at incredible speeds printing four colors into beautiful images to fool the eye and please the vision.

This cover of a portfolio for Willet Stained Gl
Studios shows a detail of a stained-glass window
a chapel of Mt. St. Joseph Academy, Erdenheim,
Color photograph by Willet Stained Glass Stud
Portfolio designed by the author.

An idea of the operation of a big multicolor press used for *letterpress* printing is shown in the above diagram. A set of curved plates is fitted to four cylinders that print yellow, red, blue, and black inks exactly in register with each other as paper feeds around a central impression cylinder. The makeready time and the heavy plates are the chief drawbacks of letterpress, but the process gains in stability and sharpness. There are also many less sophisticated presses for letterpress printing.

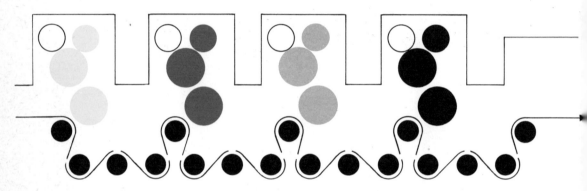

This diagram shows the four-in-line printing cylinders of a typical four-color *offset* press. Offset plates are lighter and less expensive than letterpress while makeready is faster, thus contributing to economies. The typical offset press is sheetfed—because the plates have a short life, it is difficult for a pressman to determine the number of impressions they will allow. Technical improvement has lifted offset printing from its initial use for lower-quality work to a commanding position in good printing.

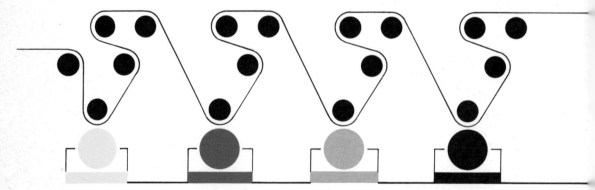

The diagram of a *gravure* printing press shows how the ink cylinders revolve in troughs of highly volatile ink. Doctor blades scrape off excess ink before the plates print on paper. Printers have long recognized that gravure printing excels in depth and range of tone, and the development of photoelectric register controls makes rotogravure capable of printing on cheap paper for newspaper, magazine, and catalog work. On the other hand some of the finest book illustrations are printed by gravure.

In letterpress printing the ink is transferred from a raised surface to the paper. A woodblock, in which areas that are not to print are gouged out, is a simple example of this technique, although letterpress plates are made of metal.

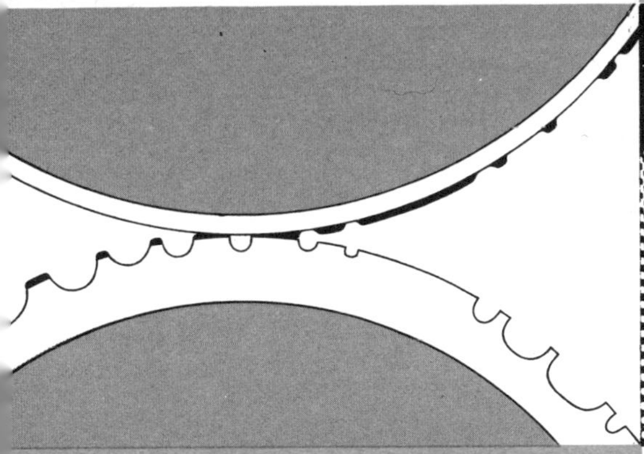

Letterpress printing ranges from linecuts through full-color plates, and some of the world's finest printing is done by this method. The enlarged section shown above is typical of a halftone screen in letterpress—the sharp impression is typical.

In offset printing an inked plate first prints against a rubber-blanket cylinder, which in turn transfers the inked image to paper. Impressions from offset are generally softer than from letterpress.

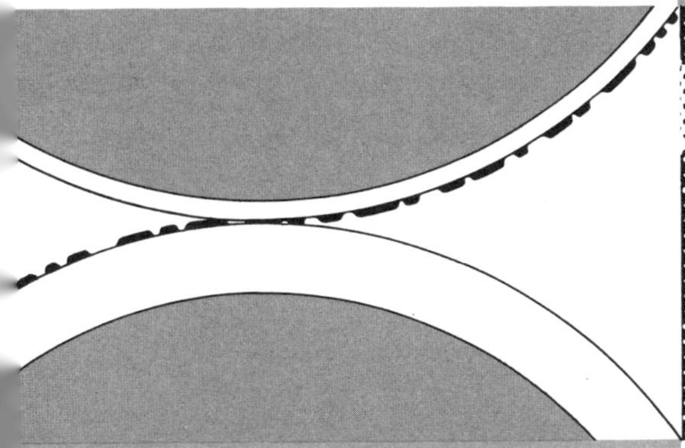

An enlarged section of an offset plate bears great resemblance to a letterpress impression. Offset papers are much faster to make and easier to handle.

In gravure printing the plate is made by coating the surface with ink and then scraping it off. The ink left in depressions in the plate is absorbed by the paper—the exact opposite of letterpress printing.

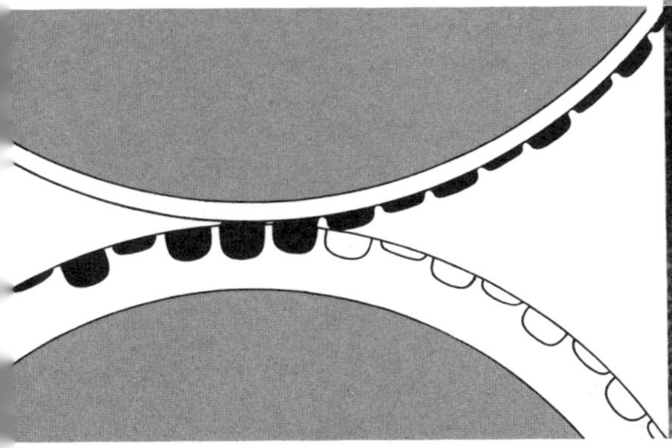

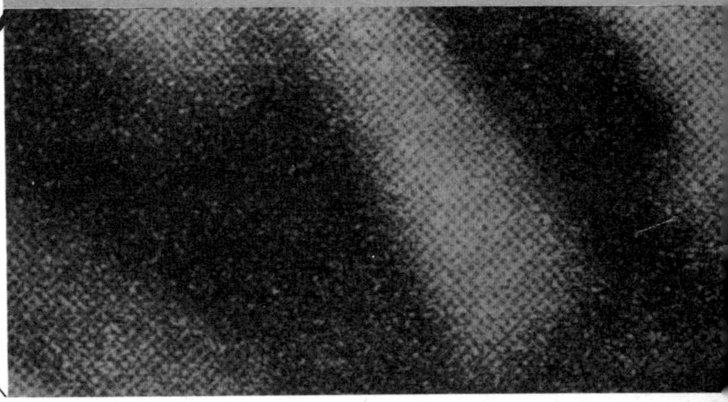

The enlargement shows the soft and subtle screen quality of a gravure plate. Fine gravure printing has a very elegant richness that is often worth the extra cost.

All color paintings, transparencies, or prints embody many different hues. In other words the originals may be considered to have a complete spectrum of color, whether they are subtle or brilliant. In reproducing the pieces the wide range of color must be reduced to only four colors: yellow, red, blue, and black. Since they are used to print the four-color process, they are known as process colors. With the exception of the black these colors are of a particular nature: the pigmentation is very standardized so that difficulties will not be encountered in achieving fidelity of color in reproductions. This is truly an amazing phenomenon—that a full sense of color can be created by printing only four colors of ink!

Original art or photography has to be photographed just as black-and-white originals do in order to make printing plates. The full range of color in the originals has to be separated through a negative process, and the results are appropriately called *separation negatives*. There are four separation negatives for a four-color reproduction, and there will ultimately be four halftone plates—one for each color—to print the projected piece.

In preparing the original for shooting the camera operator places a screen between the original and the negative. These screens, just as in shooting black-and-white halftones, break continuous tones down into dot patterns. Color filters are used for each of the four colors. However, the screens for each color must be positioned differently for each color, or else the dot patterns would fall directly on top of each other. It is essential that this does not happen, since the optical sensation of color would ultimately be lessened or even obliterated. The reproduction of an enlarged four-color piece on pages 40 and 41 shows how the screen dots are adjacent to each other. When they do print on top of each other, another color is created—blue over red becomes purple; or blue over yellow, green. The intermingling of the four colors by the screen positions is what creates the optical sensation of total full color.

In four-color printing the yellow plate is usually printed first, and the screen angle for shooting the negative is 90°.

Red is usually the second color printed, although the sequence may vary. The screen angle for the red is 75°.

The third color in the printing sequence is usually blue, and the screen angle is 105°

The black plate usually prints last, and the screen angle is 45°.

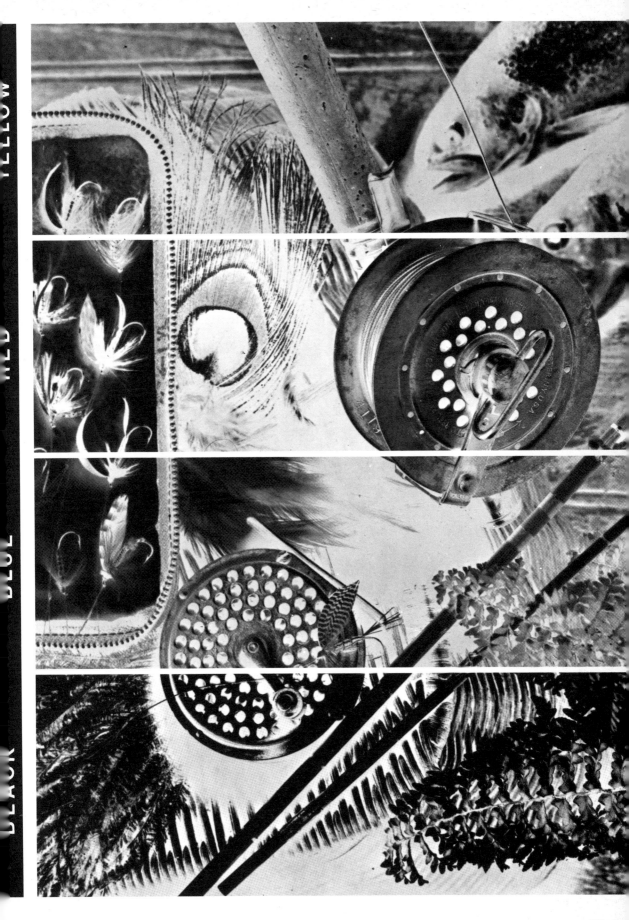

The colors of the four inks used in four-color printing are shown in the separate panels reproduced here. The total effect of the four inks printed from the four negatives in proper registration is shown in the full reproduction opposite. The proofing bars shown at the left are usually printed on the edges of each sheet as a four-color job moves through the presses. They give the pressman an opportunity to check ink flow, registration, and other details.

A four-color reproduction from a brochure entitled *The Halftone Dimension*, produced by Consolidated Papers, Inc., of Chicago.

The four-color reproduction on these pages is an enlargement of a section of the reproduction on the previous page. It shows how the dots of the four process colors (yellow, red, blue, and black) fall in a variety of patterns and in so doing fool the eye into seeing the full spectrum of color. For instance, you can detect that if blue prints over yellow, the optical sensation is of green; if blue falls on red, the optical sensation is purple. Parts of any or all of the colors falling on each other or in close proximity will produce wide variations of color. When four-color-process printing is done with normal screen sizes, the eye will not detect the screens—full-color effects will be seen as stated above. If you place an enlarging glass—a silk-thread counter (see page 10)—over the reproduction on the previous page, you will see effects similar to those shown on these pages.

It is important to point out that visual sensations resulting from the four-color process can be improved or manipulated at will by designers, engravers, and printers. First provings of color subjects are often not too good in relation to the original artwork or color photography—the effect may need to be cooler or warmer, for instance. Whatever changes or corrections may be desired can be done by the engraver on the plates or by the printer on press—or both. Good engravers, however, try to get good results as quickly as possible, for changes and corrections take time, bog down equipment, and are costly. Changes and corrections are usually absorbed by the engraver or printer if they are his responsibility; by the client, if required or instigated by him.

The Halftone Dimension

The cover of the brochure shown on page 39 is an enlargement of the four-color reproduction that page. It creates an attractive optical effect and also provides an opportunity to study the structure in a fine four-color piece. Reproduced by courtesy of Consolidated Papers, Inc.

The handsome illustration reproduced at the left is almost the extreme opposite of the subjects depicted on the previous pages. It shows the success with which four-color reproduction can capture the delicacy of a charming art subject. This full-color painting was originally printed on a soft tan paper, achieving a rich, warm effect. In this instance the paper is a much cooler white, and the effect is different but nonetheless pleasing. Many—probably at least half—of four-color subjects are printed on white paper, but the wide range of colored papers available today provides an opportunity to look for different effects. Some paper manufacturers prepare sample books of their papers in various colors on which they reproduce four-color subjects.

On page 33 is reproduced a large four-color piece, which, as it was pointed out, was taken from a very small section of a 35mm transparency. Four-color reproduction can achieve just the opposite as well. The little reproduction on the right was made from a 4"-×-5" color transparency and is an example of the fidelity that can be achieved in a small reproduction, even—in this case—of a rather dark evening scene.

Illustration from a primer on ecology produced by Southern California Edison Company, titled *The only home we have.*
Concept and design: Weller & Juett, Inc.
Project Manager: Ron Gossling, Public Information,
                           Southern California Edison Company.
Original manuscript: Ed Rabey.
Illustration: Don Weller.

From *Philadelphia USA* by Robert H. Wilson. Photography by Charles P. Mills. Published by Chilton Book Company and sponsored by Girard Bank, Philadelphia.

OTHER COLOR TECHNIQUES

The use of methods to obtain interesting color effects without the cost of four-color separation is one of the options open to the designer. Preparing four-color negatives and plates is costly and can be done only if the budget is adequate, time is available, and the *run*—the printing quantity—warrants the expense and time. For these reasons designers often rely on techniques that utilize less expensive art or photography and do not require the time and technical preparation of four-color printing.

One of these color techniques is called *overprinting*. Separation negatives are not necessary, although less complicated negatives are required. The artwork may be done in black and white only. Two, three, or more colors may be involved, and they need not be process colors—yellow, red, blue, or black—although these may be used.

The artwork used for the two-color reproduction on page 15 is shown on the opposite page—process colors were used in the reproduction. The artwork was prepared with overlays to show the engraver where the colors were to go and how they were to overprint. A colorful reproduction was achieved with a minimum of technical requirements, time, and expense.

This reproduction was made from the sa line piece as that shown on page 15 in t colors. The artwork is by Robert Milna

Although a colorful effect may be required for a reproduction, the may be no satisfactory art or photography available. In the case of reproduction shown on page 47 the client only had a poor photographic color print that had been taken under adverse conditio Time was short and the job did not call for four colors—or a four-co budget. The designer—in this case the author—asked a professio photographer to prepare a black-and-white photographic co (reproduced above) of the poor color print. Surprisingly, the bla and-white print was amazing. From it the printer made conversions his camera, obtaining a kind of separation negative that he then us to prepare the plates for the three-color reproduction in yellow, re brown, and black. This bit of technical ingenuity resulted in a f piece of printing and a happy client. In the reproduction shown he the same negatives were used, but they were printed in yellow, re and black process inks.

...terization produced by David Oser
the Oser Press for Ducon Fluid
...nsport Division of The Ducon Com-
...y, a subsidiary of United States Fil-
Corporation, King of Prussia, Pa.

Another interesting technique for achieving unusual color effects is *split-fountain* printing. The results vary enough to give a handprinted effect, but long runs are impractical. In split-fountain printing the inks are deliberately kept separate from one another but are fed to the plates at the same time. Sometimes the inks overlap on the plates, thus creating interesting nuances and gradations of color.

In the production of this book it was impossible to use a split-fountain technique. The author prepared the artwork to give the visual impression of split-fountain, and the black was simply overprinted—in effect, another example of overprinting.

PAPERMAKING

Papermaking techniques are of tremendous interest not only in themselves but as important developments in the history and advancement of culture. Despite the development of other means of communication, paper is one of the most important commodities and one that artists and designers need to know about.

The evolution of paper was gradual; the invention is credited to a Chinese court official, Ta'ai Lun, about A.D. 105. The Chinese needed a surface for calligraphy that was less expensive than the pure silk then in use and experimented with other materials such as tree bark, hemp and cotton rags, and fishnets. At first paper was used exclusively for writing; not until many years later was it used for printing—rubbings and stampings from stone seals, woodblocks, and Chinese and Korean bronze characters.

Papermaking spread from China to Korea to Japan. Paper became an important commodity in trade, and by the end of the fifth century it was in widespread use in central Asia. It took over a thousand years for papermaking to find its way to Spain and to other parts of Europe. It appears that the first European paper was made in 1276 at Fabriano, a small Italian commune, still famous for fine paper today. The Fabriano mills also claim to have originated the fine art of the watermark.

Although papermaking spread to Europe about the middle of the twelfth century, paper mills were not established in France until the early fourteenth century and in Germany fifty years later. About 1430 Switzerland, particularly Basel, became a major paper-producing center, but England's first important contribution to the industry did not come until 1495. During the eighty years culminating in the Thirty Years' War—from 1568 to 1648—Holland became a major paper-producing country.

The United States entered the scene in 1690 when William Rittenhouse and a group of influential citizens founded a mill in Germantown on the Wissahickon Creek. One of this group, William Bradford, is credited with establishing the first printing press in Pennsylvania, while Benjamin Franklin is revered to this day as the patron saint of the printing and publishing industries, particularly in Philadelphia.

This minihistory of papermaking shows that the industry got underway about three hundred years ago. Paper is now produced in countless quantities, and presses are capable of breathtaking speeds. But all of these developments were made possible by the experiments and efforts of many people years ago.

Line drawing of hemp from *Handbook of Plant and Floral Ornament* by Richard G. Hatton, Dover Publications, Inc., New York.

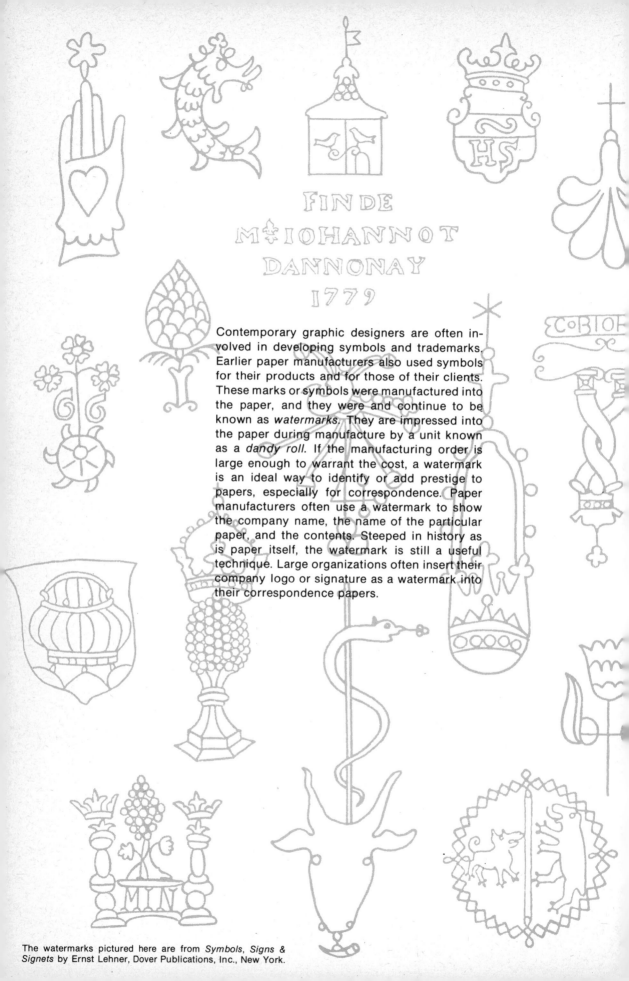

FIN DE
M⚜IOHANNOT
DANNONAY
1779

Contemporary graphic designers are often involved in developing symbols and trademarks. Earlier paper manufacturers also used symbols for their products and for those of their clients. These marks or symbols were manufactured into the paper, and they were and continue to be known as *watermarks*. They are impressed into the paper during manufacture by a unit known as a *dandy roll*. If the manufacturing order is large enough to warrant the cost, a watermark is an ideal way to identify or add prestige to papers, especially for correspondence. Paper manufacturers often use a watermark to show the company name, the name of the particular paper, and the contents. Steeped in history as is paper itself, the watermark is still a useful technique. Large organizations often insert their company logo or signature as a watermark into their correspondence papers.

The watermarks pictured here are from *Symbols, Signs & Signets* by Ernst Lehner, Dover Publications, Inc., New York.

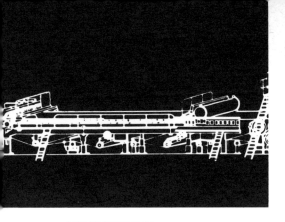

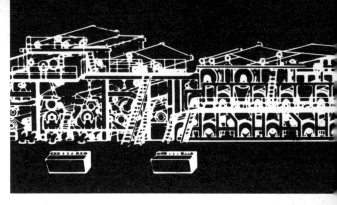

FOURDRINIER   PRESSES

Reproduced by permission from *Paper*, a publication of the T. H. Glatfelter Co., Spring Grove, Pa.

While papermaking is a fascinating subject and its history worthy of broader and deeper study, the uses of various kinds of paper for specific purposes is requisite and highly interesting information in itself.

Graphic designers are involved with paper on two levels: the papers on which artwork and designs are prepared and the papers on which designs are printed. To the designer these two concerns are inseparable. For instance, one kind of paper or board must be used for line art, another for work in watercolor or other wet media, and the papers on which such basically different art techniques are printed must be chosen just as carefully. The designer would probably specify a printing paper with a smooth surface for line art, a softer and more textured paper for watercolor.

By study and practice the designer learns about the different papers and surfaces and the purposes of charcoal papers, watercolor papers, bristol board, illustration board, papers and boards with varied surfaces such as scratchboard and coquille board, bond paper, and tissue paper. These papers are manufactured in much the same way as wrapping paper, paper bags, paperboard, writing papers, and the wide range of printing papers except that the fibers and formulas are changed according to the requirements of the end products.

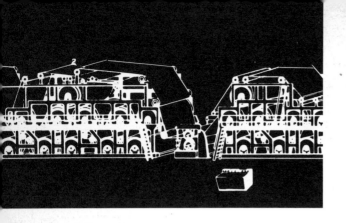 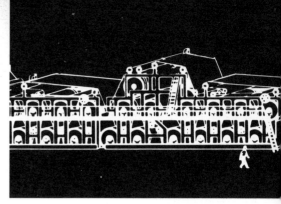

DRYERS

For the designer papers are an exciting part of his inspiration. A design library should have swatch books of samples, designer's kits, and literature about printing papers procured from paper manufacturers or their distributors. Printers also have paper samples and swatch books on file to show to designers, clients, and customers. The designer also needs paper dummies, made up by distributors or printers in the papers requested by the designer or suggested by the printer, to show to clients. They help the designer in planning a project and give the client an intelligent idea of what may be expected in the end product. They help the designer to sell and to get proper cost estimates on a job from the printer. The statement by one well-established paper manufacturer that "paper is part of the picture" is almost a cliché but nevertheless very true.

Without going into detail on the nomenclature of trade-name papers, it is important to mention briefly the types of paper with which designers are invariably concerned. The character and quality, thickness or thinness of a paper are manufactured for specific printing needs. It is obvious that the paper required for a newspaper is not the same as that required for a quality magazine. The following is a brief description of important paper types and their uses.

A modern papermaking machine in a plant of Champion Papers, Inc.

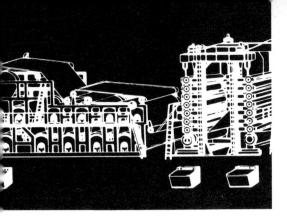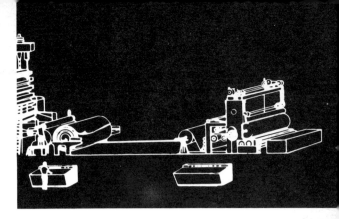

CALENDERS   REEL   REWINDER

Newsprint is a low-grade paper of adequate quality for the average newspaper. Designers sometimes use it to create an effect.

Kraft is a coarse paper, available in several colors, which is sometimes used for effect or to create the impression of low cost (which is not always the case).

Parchment is traditionally used for diplomas, citations, and the like but is now manufactured for many creative uses as well. It is very effective as an overlay on maps, charts, and plans and for see-through visual effects in the graphic arts.

Bond and *mimeograph* papers are manufactured for office and correspondence purposes. They come in a variety of weights, textures, and colors. Envelopes are usually available in matching colors and textures and in popular sizes.

Text, *cover*, and *bristol* papers are available in a wide range to accommodate the equally wide range of printing needs. Text weights are usually used for the interior pages; cover weights, obviously, for covers. Bristol weights are often used for mailing cards. All come in matching colors and textures. The variety of text and cover papers has broadened tremendously in the past few years, offering a stimulating selection of exciting colors and textures.

Duplex papers are usually white on one side with a choice of colors on the other side. They are actually two sheets of text or cover paper glued together. They offer interesting possibilities to designers, but their use must be weighed against the comparative cost of printing a color.

Cast-coated papers, usually cover weight, are coated on one side with a shiny pigment that is available in a variety of colors. They offer exciting design possibilities.

In addition to the basic information outlined above there are other factors to be considered by people who work with printing papers. All paper manufacturers use brand names, which are their marketing labels and which almost always include the grade. A paper's name and characteristics might be presented in this manner, for example: PAPERCO Sandstone Offset Vellum 70# Text. PAPERCO denotes the manufacturer's name (fictitious); sandstone, the color; offset, the type of printing it is designed for; vellum*, the finish; 70# text, the basis weight (# or lb.) or substance weight (sub.), which are interchangeable. *The surfaces of printing papers can be divided into two main classifications—*uncoated* and *coated*. Uncoated papers have good body and strength, a quality feel, and glareproof characteristics. Coated papers have a compact, tight feel, a high-quality look, and a surface on which ink colors stand out sharply.

Text papers, as mentioned above, are suitable for the inside pages of a booklet or book (and may be suitable for other uses). *Book* papers are actually text papers with a much lighter basis weight. Heavier papers, which may be of the same character and quality as a given text paper, are called *cover* papers. The paper specifications for a booklet might be, for instance, 80# cover and 70# text, and it might be spoken of as "24 pages and cover." If the cover has the same basis weight as the text pages, it is referred to as *self-cover*.

Papermaker's swatch books usually include detailed charts that delineate all the characteristics of a particular paper. This information is essential to printers, who continually refer to them to find out the weights, textures, and sizes of sheets available—very important in relation to the sizes of the presses. Since papermakers are eager for designers to use these swatch books, you should become familiar with them in order to work intelligently with printers. A fine design deserves a fine paper—the stereotyped statement "just as good" is not acceptable.

TEXT MILL STOCK ITEMS

BASIS 25 x 38

| | 80 lb. | 100 lb. Sheets | Basis 20 x 26 |

Basis 25 x 38   50   60 lb   70 lb

COLORS			BASIC		50 lb				ream wt	wt/M shts	shts/ctn	rms/skd	ream wt
SIZE	Ream Wt.										5000		6.88
8½ x 11	4.									5.90	11.80	2500		13.76
8½ x 14	6									11.80	23.60	2200		29
11 x		finish	color	stock sizes	grain	ream wt	wt/M shts	shts/ctn	rms/skd	5000				
17½ x 2														
19 x 2				8½ x 11 ●●	L									
23 x 2		smooth	white	11 x 17 ●●	L									
23 x 3				17½ x 22½	L									
25 x 38				19 x 25	L									
28 x 42				22½ x 35	L									
35 x 45				23 x 29 ■	L									
38 x 50				23 x 35 ■	L									
NOTE: All it				25 x 38 ■	L									
				28 x 42	L									
				28 x 44	L									
				32 x 44 ■	L									
				35 x 45 ■	I									

STANDARD SIZES • WEIGHT PER REAM
CONSULT MERCHANT CATALOG FOR ITEMS CARRIED IN LOCAL STOCK

BASIS 25 x 38	70		80	
			56	(1300)
23 x 29	49	(1600)	68	(1100)
23 x 35	59½	(1200)	80	(1000)
25 x 38	70	(1000)	133	(600)
	116	(600)		

Swatch and sample books, some of which are shown on these pages, are absolute must for the graphic designer. They can be obtained simply by as either the paper manufacturer or a large distributor in your locality. Practic designers are visited quite regularly by these representatives, who know designers are very influential in making selections for their projects. paper swatch books shown here are from some of the major paper manu turers, and the author considers them an important part of his graphic library. They are essential in supplying information about weights, textu colors, and sizes, often demonstrate interesting facts about printing prod tion, and certainly stimulate the imagination.

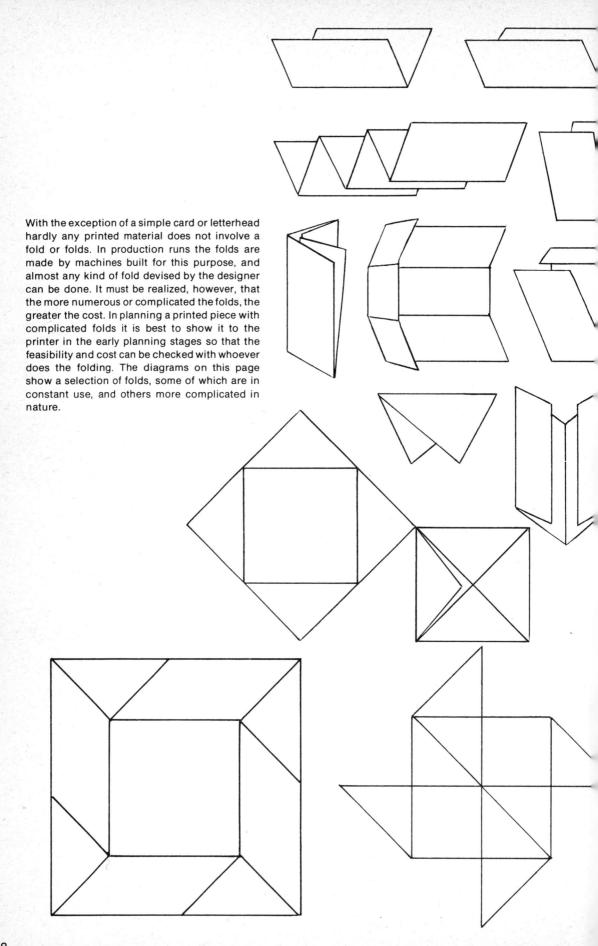

With the exception of a simple card or letterhead hardly any printed material does not involve a fold or folds. In production runs the folds are made by machines built for this purpose, and almost any kind of fold devised by the designer can be done. It must be realized, however, that the more numerous or complicated the folds, the greater the cost. In planning a printed piece with complicated folds it is best to show it to the printer in the early planning stages so that the feasibility and cost can be checked with whoever does the folding. The diagrams on this page show a selection of folds, some of which are in constant use, and others more complicated in nature.

svdwfb arfegs. Akdfh tkowhd adhbsw yudrqp idrh
oyxwsr; kawomc rdubkh tziurq. Eawoc falhy svljat
udghbr ebagok clyrho. Yogbc ydktc djfinr htbls fjr
rgimwa hsidyf naitof yfdhgc griyf vulcft kaym arbf
arfg odwk ilyq nupj thmb escv. Romv idfb nlwg ah;

Pictured here is an exploratory project in which a large square of paper is folded into a triangular form. A piece such as this one would certainly make an intriguing unit for a direct-mail presentation. However, it is complicated from a manufacturing standpoint and would probably cause problems in mailing. Nevertheless, this kind of exploratory exercise is important for the designer to attempt, since it is his job to make every piece he designs as inviting or interesting as possible.

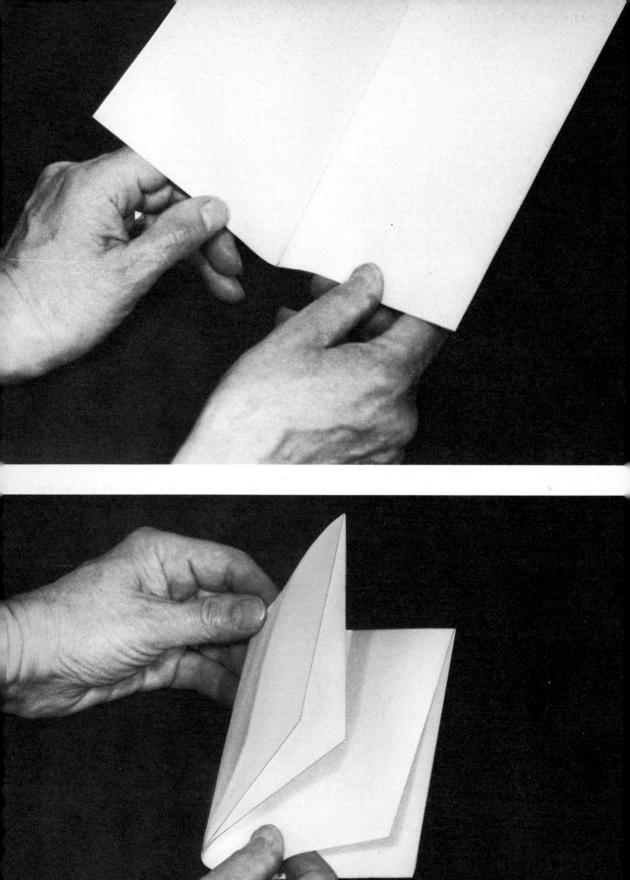

The first fold of a sheet of paper creates four pages.
The second fold creates eight pages.
The third fold creates sixteen pages.

A great deal of printing is done on a single sheet of paper, either on the front only or on the front and back. If the printed piece is to be more than a single sheet, it is prepared in multiples of 4, 8, or 16 pages, known as *forms*. Forms or pages are printed on one large sheet of paper, folded to the required number and order of pages, and trimmed. A piece of 48 pages, for example, may be printed in three 16-page forms. If you examine some books carefully, you may be able to determine how many forms were printed to make the total number of pages.

These forms, of course, can be printed in one color, two or more colors, or four-color process. In most instances one side of the sheet is printed first, then turned and fed through the press to print the other side. The technical term for this is *work-and-turn*. Sometimes for the sake of economy one color (say, black) is printed on one side of the form, and black and another color on the other side. This is not always true because some presses can handle two or more colors economically with a long run.

The exercise in folding paper shown here will help you determine how color is or is not printed. In this example one side of a 16-page form is one-color, and the other side is two-color. Folding a flat sheet of paper once creates 4 pages; a second fold creates 8 pages; a third fold creates 16 pages. Color markings are placed on the panels created on one side of the sheet to determine which pages carry the second color. Trimming all edges except the central fold creates a dummy booklet. This information is useful to know in preparing designs.

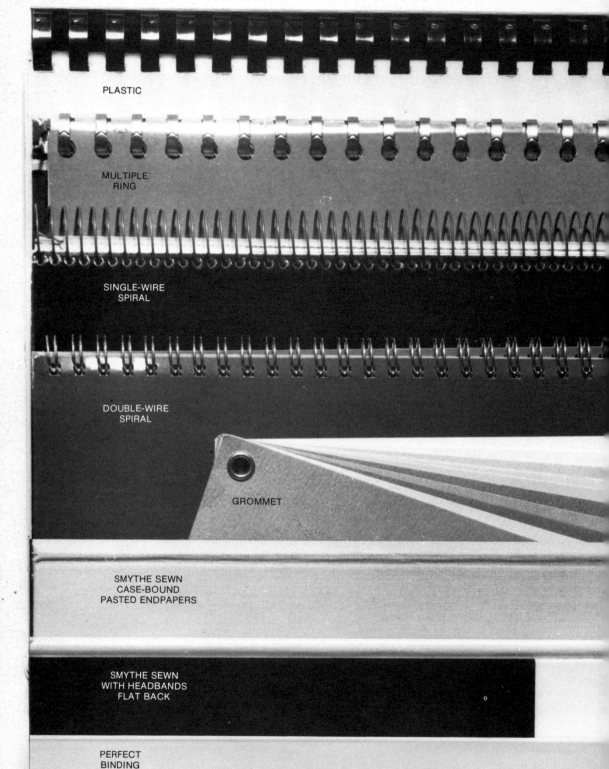

PLASTIC

MULTIPLE
RING

SINGLE-WIRE
SPIRAL

DOUBLE-WIRE
SPIRAL

GROMMET

SMYTHE SEWN
CASE-BOUND
PASTED ENDPAPERS

SMYTHE SEWN
WITH HEADBANDS
FLAT BACK

PERFECT
BINDING

STAPLE

Other types of binding are available. The group
shown here suggests the variety of possible uses.

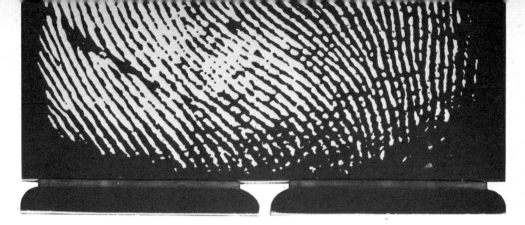

DING

ost projects the designer does not need to
der a binding, since the piece may simply be
d or, in the case of several pages, stapled.
 are, however, many situations in which bind-
 required, and the type of binding selected
s the aesthetics, the structure, the efficient
nd the life of the project.
he weight of the paper and the number of
 allow, a neat fold for a booklet or stapling a
ure is a satisfactory solution. But as a printed
 becomes thicker and heavier as more pages
ded, other forms of binding must be used,
 as *perfect* binding, in which all of the folds
ued and neatly squared off. A book or catalog
ed to open easily and lie flat calls for wire or
c. Sample books are often bound with grom-
so that the pages may be turned for side-by-
comparisons. Catalogs and price lists, from
 pages are frequently removed or changed,
 a loose-leaf treatment.

An unusually ingenious binding on a
small German catalog of artists' work
entitled *Preistrager 1955, Helmut
Lorz, Wilhelm Loth* by Darmstadter
Kunstpreis.

Enlarged cross-section of perfect
binding showing ten forms in
white paper and two forms in
colored paper bound with a
cover-weight stock.

ding properly specified
 manufactured enhances
earance of a printed piece
nds its lifetime of beauty
fulness. The illustration
 left shows a variety of
methods. Occasionally an
tive binding such as the
tured at the top of this
developed.
utside fold of the binding
ece of printed matter is
 as the *spine*, and the
 where the pages come
r is called the *gutter*.
 the most common sins
ted by designers and
rs of printed material is
ion type matter so close
gutter that the book al-
s to be cracked in order
it. This is done too often,
here is an ample or even
vide margin at the other
he page. The purpose of
g a piece of reading
 is to entice the reader
make it possible for him
 the contents. This kind
elessness should be

SPECIAL TECHNIQUES

There are other techniques available to the designer which allow greater latitudes of expression in creating intriguing pieces. These include embossing and debossing, engraving, die-cutting, stamping, and, in the final stages of multiple-page pieces, collating.

The dictionary gives several meanings for *embossing*. Perhaps it can be stated most simply by saying that it is a process whereby designs or letters are raised on an otherwise flat surface by means of pairs of dies, one the negative of the other. Embossing is used on letterheads, booklets, or reports, often combined with other printing—the resulting effect can be one of quality or prestige. *Debossing* is simply the reverse of this procedure—the impression is indented *into* the paper. Embossing has been overused in the past several years as a stock method of gaining a prestige look. It can and often does do this, but it is not the only design criterion for the prestige effect. Embossing adds to the cost of a printed piece in relation to the intricacy of the dies that must be made.

Engraving is another printing technique that is often used to create the effect of a special occasion—for instance, engraved invitations—or special prestige—business cards, calling cards, or letterheads. Good engraving is usually done by special printers and it is not to be compared with contemporary techniques that simulate engraving but are not as excellent.

Die-cutting, appropriately used, certainly adds to the interest of a printed piece and is often employed in direct-mail design. The technique of die-cutting is almost self-evident: a die is prepared, which is actually a piece of sharp metal formed to the contours of the cut and set into a block of wood, and is then used in a machine to cut the forms as required for the design. Because making a cutting die requires time and technical skill, this process adds to the expense. In many cases the cost is no doubt offset by the attention it attracts.

Stamping is a process that creates a very shiny effect—for instance, a line drawing stamped in silver or gold into almost any color of paper is very effective. The process involves a combination of a plate, heat, and pressure, and the resultant image is actually pressed (indented) into the paper. Printing gold or silver inks cannot compare with the shining impression achieved by gold or silver stamping.

Collating is not related to the techniques described above, since it has nothing to do with printing as such, but it does add another decorative possibility to design. The term refers to the order in which printed sheets are collected or arranged in a booklet, book, or other printed piece. The designer may plan a project so that a printed piece has forms on different kinds of paper. As an example, in annual reports of large organizations the text about the general activities of the company may be printed on fine white paper (perhaps with four-color reproductions), but the financial matter may be printed on paper with an entirely different color and texture. The two papers, properly planned and collated, increase the visual interest of a report and organize the material for more effective evaluation.

The reproductions on this and the following two pages show effective uses of embossing and debossing. Embossing is most often used on white paper, as in the soft-bound book cover below. Fine examples of embossing can be done on colored papers—on page 67 embossing and black stamping were used on a black cover stock for an altogether unusual effect.

The foregoing might suggest that embossing is effective only with lettered or geometric forms. The example on page 66 shows that drawn forms—sometimes quite intricate—are entirely possible.

The embossed cover of a book derived from an exhibition presented in the Library of Congress, Washington, D.C., which opened on April 21, 1968. The cover is reproduced by permission of the Library of Congress.

WESTERN AIR LINES INC. 1967 ANNUAL REPORT

Cover embossing for a Western Airlines, Inc., annual rep

CRUM & FORSTER   1972 Annual Report

Cover of Crum & Forster annual report.
Designed by Graphic Images, Inc.

CRUM & FORSTER

The form of an envelope before folding and gluing is the result of a die-cut operation, although the completed product is a simple rectangle or square. The contents of an envelope may be a simple letter or as unusual as the items shown here, all of which were made more intriguing by the use of die-cutting.

The bars on the circus spread are die-cut, as can be seen by the shadow cast in photographing it. On the small mailing piece at the far left the outlines of the flower are die-cut and folded to create a pocket into which the flat piece with the hummingbird is slipped. Die-cuts have also been employed in the portfolio for four booklets shown at the bottom left.

This double-page spread of a tiger and bars is shown by courtesy of Champion Papers, Inc., and is from *Imagination II*, one of a series of distinguished publications produced by the company.

Die-cut mailing piece (hummingbird and flower) entitled *Some things you can't put a price on* is reproduced by courtesy of Hammermill Paper Company.

The portfolio for the Thomas Jefferson University Sesquicentennial Campaign was designed by the author.

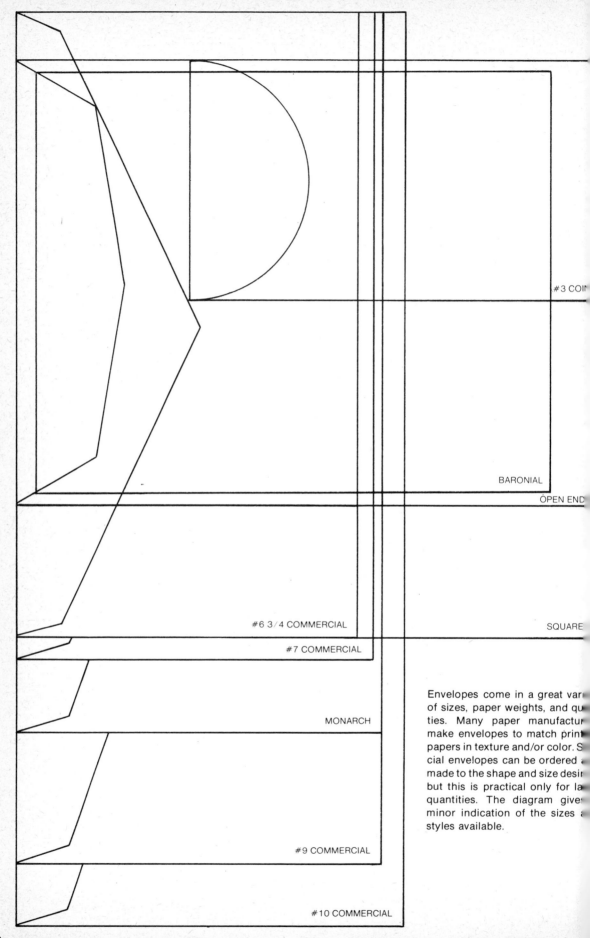

#3 COIN

BARONIAL

OPEN END

#6 3/4 COMMERCIAL

SQUARE

#7 COMMERCIAL

MONARCH

Envelopes come in a great var
of sizes, paper weights, and qu
ties. Many paper manufactu
make envelopes to match print
papers in texture and/or color. S
cial envelopes can be ordered
made to the shape and size desir
but this is practical only for la
quantities. The diagram give
minor indication of the sizes
styles available.

#9 COMMERCIAL

#10 COMMERCIAL

...merican West Publishing Company.
...signer: George Pfeiffer III.
...otographer: David Cavagnaro.

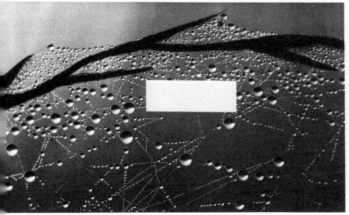

Champion Papers, Inc., *Imagination XVII*, on Australia.

Most envelopes are utilitarian—and dull. With some imagination they can invite the recipient to at least take a look inside. In some instances this can be done at very little cost, for negatives of art used in the printed insert may be employed. The examples shown here and others like them challenge designers to create more interesting envelopes.

The Children's Hospital of Philadelphia.

New insights into a world of genius—
THE UNKNOWN LEONARDO

Horizon Books, McGraw-Hill.

...can Heritage Publishing Co., Inc.

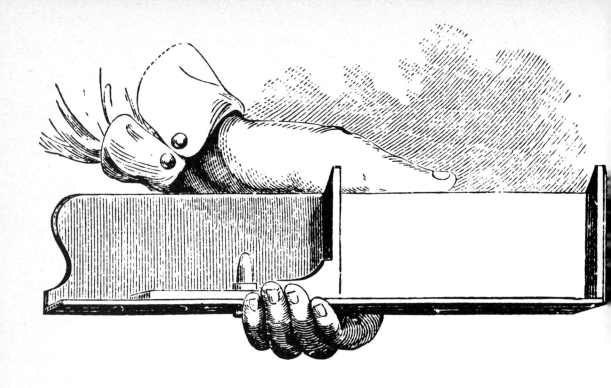

LETTERS AND TYPE

Good design demands an excitement about letterforms, from hand-drawn letters to contemporary computerized type. Unless a designer feels this excitement about the uses of letters and type, his work is generally doomed to dullness and mediocrity.

There are many interesting and informative books about the alphabet, some on the history of letters, others on construction and usage, many on type and typography. Books on these subjects should be a part of every graphic-arts library. On the other hand, today's designer is besieged with offerings of type styles and other do-it-yourself forms that make it easy to become trapped in set patterns of thought and application.

Somehow both ends of the alphabetic spectrum must be kept alive. To explain this thought, turn to the reproduction of the menu cover on page 17. This design *could* have been set in type; it also could have been done in the ubiquitous calligraphic style that has recently entrapped the educational world. Instead the designer chose to use an explosive, contemporary, individualized script, with immensely intriguing results.

Typesetting has undergone many changes in the past 100 years or so. In the mid-1800s the standard method of setting type was with a hand-held stick, as shown above. Each unit of type was taken from a case, as shown in the old illustration at the top right. Note that the typographer is standing in front of a bench on which is an upper and a lower typecase. Capital letters are traditionally held in the upper case and small letters in the lower case, thus the terminology of *uppercase* (capital letters) and *lowercase* (small letters). Typesetting by hand from cases such as these is still done, and, because the typesetter has complete control, very excellent work may result.

Over the years speedier methods of setting type have been developed, and monotype and linotype have held a prime position in the printing crafts. Type is literally made from molten metal on monotype and linotype machines; the operator types on a huge keyboard in much the same way as on a typewriter. Type set on these machines is commonly called *hot-metal type*. Type set on typewriterlike machines with special fonts is commonly called *cold type*—the type is *on* the machine, just like a regular typewriter—no heat is involved.

Earlier in this book the importance of the camera in graphic-reproduction techniques was emphasized. It is just as important in typesetting. Setting type photographically is now commonplace, and, coupled with computerization, the speed and excellence of type set in this manner are breathtaking. At the far right a type font—filmstrip—for computerized photographic typesetting is shown. The operator uses a keyboard, and the filmstrip is scanned by a beam of light as the selected letters are punched by the operator. This operation is extremely fast.

Young graphic designers should make a point of visiting important typographic organizations (unless it was a part of their professional training in a good design college) to become aware of the various activities involved in setting type. This is a great help in visualizing what happens to a project and in being able to specify type material precisely. Some design colleges have typographic and printing equipment with which their students may work—this is an excellent opportunity to get the feel of typesetting and printing.

Typesetting equipment is manufactured by many organizations in the United States and abroad, and type designers have contributed their talents over the years to the vast variety of type styles available. The reproduction on the right shows how four fonts of type are contained on filmstrips used in the typesetting equipment manufactured by the Compugraphic Corporation of Wilmington, Massachusetts. Courtesy of Walter Andrews Associates, Philadelphia.

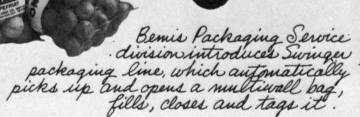

The Visinet Mill (St. Louis) expands polypropylene film extrusion capabilities, enabling production all the yarn required for its continuing conversion to synthetic fiber open-mesh fabrics.

Bemis Packaging Service division introduces Swinger packaging line, which automatically picks up and opens a multiwall bag, fills, closes and tags it.

Annual meeting of stockholders is held at the First National Bank of Boston. Company announces record capital expenditure program.

D. A. Clarke, corporate director of public and A. L. Park, director of personnel and industrial relations, elected corporate vice presidents.

Four Mankato Corp.-produced boxes win two first awards and five Excellence awards in various categories of the International Rigid Paper Box Association competition.

Cover of *Visionary Cities: The Arcology of Paolo Soleri*,
by Donald R. Wall.
Graphic design by Donald R. Wall and Walter Borek.
© 1971 by Praeger Publishers, Inc., New York.
Reprinted by permission.

The two pieces reproduced here, both excellent in quality, are about as far apart in the use of letterforms as possible. On the left a page from an annual report uses a legible handwriting instead of type, thus creating in a publication distributed to employees and stockholders a sense of personal contact.

The cover design above uses type forms in a collagelike manner, suggesting the very contemporary approach of the book.

from an annual report of the Bemis Company.
and designer: Runsey, Lundquist & Associates,
        Foshay Tower, Minneapolis.

THE SPECIFICATION OF TYPE

*Helvetica Med
10 pt Caps
letter spaced to
16 picas*

*Helvetica 9 pt C+L.C.
2 pt leaded X 22 picas
flush L+r.*

Although he will seldom write text for a project the
designer will be furnished with typewritten material
for which he will specify the type to be set as a
part of his design work. In order that his specifications (specs) may be followed correctly by a typographer he should insist that the material he receives
be neatly and correctly typed and double-spaced.

*10 pt. l.
betwee
all pa*

Specifications for setting in type have been indicated on this material exactly as it would be done on an
actual job. The more complicated the job the more
careful and detailed the specifications must be.

*Helvetica
9 pt. C+L.
3 pt lead
X 22 p
flush L*

It must be emphatically stated that in the rising
costs of today's typesetting "specs" must be clear,
accurate and every possibility for error avoided.

In most type jobs it is normal to call for "galley"
proof that these be proofread for errors,
ons and/or deletions after which reproduction
proofs are requested. The "repro" proofs are used
for the designer's mechanicals for the printer. Most
type houses supply a minimum of three or four "repros"
as a precaution against mistakes or smudging while
the art mechanicals are being prepared.

*Helvetica
Itals
8 pt C+L.C.
1 pt leaded
X 22 picas*

Note: The number of errors and
setting ~~on the opposite~~ *of this text*
tings, if the ori
have foll
de

HELVETICA with Medium

SPECIMEN ALPHABET
ABCDEFGHIJKLMNOPQRSTUVWXYZ
ABCDEFGHIJKLMNOPQRSTUVWXYZ
abcdefghijklmnopqrstuvwxyz fi fl ff ffi ffl
abcdefghijklmnopqrstuvwxyz fi fl ff ffi ffl
1234567890$
%
7/8 2/3 %
5/8 1/3 2/3
1/8 1/3
~~890$~~ Œ Œ

JCM

LINO

LINOTYPE

MONO-FOUNDRY

PICAS
INCHES
50
45
40

The commonly accepted symbols shown below are used to mark up typewritten copy with the *specifications* (specs) for typesetting and to indicate corrections on galley proofs. The first typesetting proofs are known as *galley proofs* and are usually furnished on low-quality paper and not in page form or composition. Proofreader's corrections or changes are usually marked in red ink on the galleys to catch the attention of the typesetter. Designers should remember—and so advise clients—that typed copy for setting should be as accurate as possible and that the specs to the typographer should be complete and explicit. Typographers do an amazingly accurate job of setting type as specified and their errors (PEs—printer's errors) are corrected at no cost to the client, *but* changes or errors made by the client or the designer (AAs—author's alterations) are charged and are often expensive. After galley corrections are made and approved, the typesetter furnishes *reproduction proofs* (repros), which are, as the name implies, in camera-ready form and are pasted up on the final art mechanics.

Symbol	Meaning	Symbol	Meaning	Symbol	Meaning
℘	delete (take out)	⊐	move to right	⎯em	1 em dash
⊃⊂	close up	⊏	move to left	⎯en	1 en dash
℘	delete and close up	☐	indent 1 em	ꙅ	turn inverted letter
#	insert space	¶	make paragraph	⏝	push down space
Eq. #	equal space	no ¶	no paragraph	stet	keep as is
less #	less space	wf	wrong font letter	caps	capitals
∧	insert at this point	⊙	period	S.C.	small capitals
ld in⟩	insert lead between lines	⋏	comma	bf	set boldface
(/)	parentheses	⋏	semicolon	lc	set lowercase
[/]	insert brackets	⋏	colon	ital	set italics
✗	defective letter or type	⋎	apostrophe	⟨?⟩	query
Rom.	set in roman type	⋎ | ⋎	quotation marks	sp	spell out
=	straighten lines	=|	insert hyphen	⊓	raise
‖	align type	tr ⌐	transpose	⊔	lower

The Case of the Missing Comma

Correcting text after it has been set is a time-consuming and costly procedure. To add or delete a *comma* on a typewritten sheet is a simple matter (and that is where it should be done); on a typeset sheet it is something else altogether. Here is what has to be done.

1. The change is phoned to the type house.
2. It is entered on a time sheet and sent to the composing room.
3. An operator may be forced to interrupt another job; he removes a magazine from the machine and replaces it with one holding the correct type for the comma.
4. Seven machine adjustments are made.
5. He sets a new line (or paragraph) including the required comma.
6. The line is cleaned, proofed, and sent to a reader for OK.
7. The new line (or paragraph) is sent to a compositor. He must find the location of the page form to be corrected.
8. He finds the form, unties the previously set type, and inserts the new line.
9. A proof with the new comma is pulled.
10. The proof is sent to a reader to check the new line for accuracy, proper position, and spacing.
11. A new set of revised repros is pulled.
12. The page form is washed and returned to storage.
13. Revised repro proofs are sent to the customer.
14. Time records are entered, and the charges are added to the customer's invoice.

All for the want of a *comma*. This rather droll story has been kicking around in graphic circles for some time—the author's identity is lost. It points up just how much effort goes into unnecessary typesetting changes and why they cost so much. In actual practice a good graphic designer might be able to cut a missing comma from an extra repro sheet and paste it into position.

Pop goes the Weasel!

HIPPODROME

COME, MY LOVE, MY DEAREST.

BOSTON:
$7,821. &

Ida May

The letterforms shown here are typical of old music sheets and type-specimen books. There has recently been a great revival of forms such as these, particularly in photolettering and transfer-lettering techniques. The use of these readily procurable letterforms adds to the variety of styles that designers have at their command, particularly for titles and headlines.

MODERN DIDOT

MODERN DIDOT

MODERN DIDOT

MODERN DIDOT

MODERN DIDOT

MODERN DIDOT

MODERN DIDOT

MODERN DIDOT

MODERN DIDOT

MODERN DIDOT

MODERN DIDOT

Process letters, much in use today, are letterforms manufactured in negative form on film. They are available in a vast variety of styles and can be ordered in any reasonable size. Specimen sheets are available, and designers can order the style desired by a key number. Their selections can be made into headlines or set to follow a design layout, and they will receive a positive or negative print that follows the specifications. If they are ordered to the exact size required, these prints can be pasted in position on art mechanicals.

ELVETICA

ELVETICA

ELVETICA

ELVETICA

ELVETICA

DORADO

DORADO

EVINNE

EVINNE

PLOMAT

STER

ENTURY
OLDSTYLE HEAVY

OMANO

LE ROBUR

BAVARIAN

STENCIL

BARNUM

PLAYBILL

FLORIDORA

CARNIVAL

BOOKMAN

BOOKMAN

CHELTENHAM

LATIN

ANTIQUE LATIN

GOUDY HEAVY

RIVIERA

ROYCROFT

FRENCH LATIN

DE VINNE

PEIGNOT

BRITANNIC

PLANTIN

MASTODON

AD GOTHIC

RUBENS

DELLA ROBBIA

Tempus DESIGN

Tempus DESIGN

These pages show some of the immense variety of letter-forms available from Techni-Process, Inc., reproduced here by courtesy of Typographic Service, Inc., of Philadelphia.

The examples on this page do not begin to show the scope and variety of forms available in process letters. The selections of Modern Didot suggest the great variety that can be obtained even in one typeface. The other three columns indicate in a very small way the variety of styles and the positive and negative forms that may be specified.

Annlie Extra

Alternate Gothic No.

Annlie Extra

Annonce

Berling Bold

Antique Olive

Beton Medium

Avant Garde

Bookman

Avant Garde

Carousel

Cable Heavy

Caslon 540

Compacta Light

Caslon Black

Compacta Bold

Century

eurostile

Clarendon

eurostile

Egyptienne

americar

Melior

Blanchard

Modern No. 20

Bottleneck

Times Bold

CHARRETT

Other letterforms that were developed recently and are much used today are dry *trans-fer letters*. They come on transparent sheets with an adhesive backing protected by a slip sheet, and (after the slip sheet is removed) they can be transferred to roughs, comps, visual aids, or finished artwork by simple pressure, as shown in the illustration at the right. As with process letters, the selections are numerous and are only suggested by the examples shown here. Several companies manufacture transfer type.

The examples shown here are by courtesy of Letra-set USA Inc., one of the major producers of dry-transfer letters and other graphic-arts materials.

rhold Böcklin   Grotesque 9

ISTRA   Grotesque 9 Ital

vant Garde   Grotesque 215

vant Garde   Grotesque 211

ABY TEETH   Helvetica Extra

EANS   Helvetica Ligh

INNER   Helvetica Me

LOOK UP   B

OMBERE

RAINDING

LLION

SORAI

YSTER

able Ligh

ALY

amellia

aslon

aslon 54

irkulus

t ie medium

Letraset 72pt HELVETICA MEDIUM

AABCC
EEEEE
HIIJK
NNOOR
RRRSSS
TUUUVVW
AAABBCC
EEEEEE
IIIJKLII
OOD
M

WORKING WITH PICTURES

In addition to the art equipment and supplies usually found in a graphic-arts studio, some of which are shown on pages 98 and 99, certain instruments are necessary for sizing and cropping artwork and photographs used in art mechanicals. The circular object pictured on this page is called a *proportion guide*, and it is essential for determining the correct relationship between the size of an original and the desired enlargement or reduction of the reproduction. Situations such as the following often occur. Say you have a piece of art that measures 12″ in width and 8¼″ in height and that must be reduced to 8½″ in width. To prepare the mechanical correctly, you may need to know the reduced height dimension. Proper usage of the proportion guide will determine that it is 5 13/16″. Enlargements can be determined in the same manner.

The long object shown on this page is a graphic-arts ruler, which is imprinted on both sides with data and references useful to the designer. On the facing side are a *density guide*, sometimes called a *screen-tint finder*, which is very useful in determining the desired percentage for either black-and-white or color reproduction; a halftone-screen guide; and markings in inches and picas. The reverse side often contains charts and information about type usage.

Both of these instruments and other useful graphic-arts tools are available at most art- or drafting-supply stores.

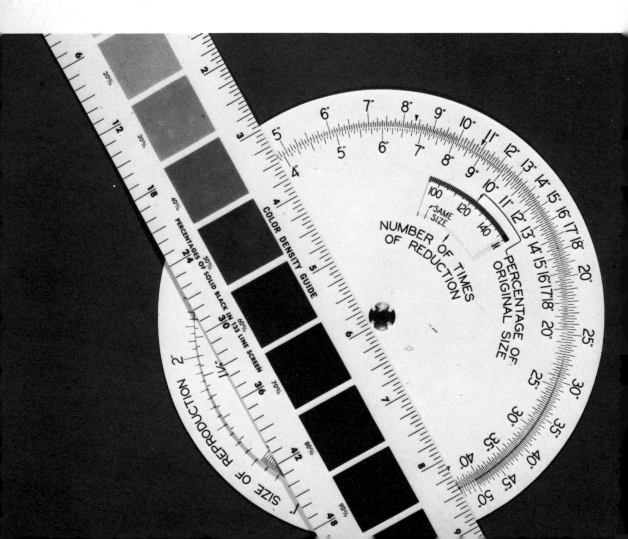

There is no greater untruth than the statement that "the camera never lies." In the hands of competent designers, photographers, retouchers, platemakers, and other technical people a completely plausible photograph may have been drastically altered en route to final reproduction. On pages 46 and 47 it is shown how an extremely inferior photograph was manipulated to make a striking three-color reproduction that serves its purpose well. A situation such as this is far from ideal—one of the greatest scourges in the graphic arts is an individual who takes an inferior picture with an equally inferior camera and requires that it has to be used because it is "all he has."

Nevertheless, there are certain techniques that a designer may want to apply to even the finest photographic material for very proper though undetected reasons. These techniques include sizing, cropping, flopping, silhouetting or outlining, retouching, the use of high- or low-key prints, negative prints, and all of the halftone and duotone procedures described earlier in this book.

Sizing and *cropping* of artwork and photographs are basic and constant elements in the preparation of printed material. Artists and illustrators often need to prepare their originals on a larger scale than the final reproductions, and photographers seldom finish their prints (enlargements) to the actual reproduction size. It is necessary for the designer using these originals to indicate to the engraver and the printer exactly how much they are to be enlarged or reduced and exactly where they are to be trimmed (or cropped) to fit the required space on a margin or a *bleed page*—a page on which reproduced material, such as photographs, art, or panels, extends off the edge at the top, bottom, and/or sides.

The reproductions shown on pages 24 and 25 demonstrate the importance of intelligent retouching and silhouetting. The following pages show several suggestions as to how photographs can be manipulated to make them more useful for various purposes. The need or the aesthetics of an assignment often dictates the approach to be taken.

s photograph was shot in a mu-
m, and the surroundings, which
not add to the beauty of the ob-
, had to be included. The contact
t is reproduced at the right.

The top of this French dormer window bears the arms of Jeanne de Balzac and comes from the Chateau de Montal, built by her around 1523. Reproduced by courtesy of the Victoria and Albert Museum, London.

Special cropping or masking often improves the impression of a photograph. This reproduction shows how cropping (on the left) eliminates details that interfere with the elegant beauty of the sculptured piece. Masking out the background enhances the detail even more. Amberlith or Rubylith is excellent for masking purposes. These are trade names for acetates to which a thin, semitransparent pink or red sheet is adhered, which may be cut away and lifted with a studio knife. The mask defines the exact area of the reproduction.

RASOIR ELEC
REMING
LE PLUS R

EN
VENTE

ici

B:
H
BL

3 5/16"

Reducing and enlarging, cropping and sizing are constants in the graphic designer's activities. Artwork is often prepared to the proper proportions, although it may be larger or smaller than the desired reproduction. A photograph is seldom taken of only the desired details. As an example, in the photographs on these pages the pair of scissors was the only object of interest. The telephone poles and buildings on the left were unimportant, as was the sign to the right of the scissors.

Typical crop marks (meaning *cut* or *trim*) are shown on the page at the left, as well as the sizing (dimensions) desired. The finished reproduction at the top right of this page is the result, an interesting composition with unusual proportions.

The photographic negative is shown below right, the contact print above, and the enlargement above right.

There are cases in which a very light or high-key effect is needed in a halftone reproduction, often to allow for type overprinting the picture. In the photograph reproduced here the negative had a normal exposure, but a very light enlargement was called for. This effect can also be achieved by the printer when he shoots the negative for the halftone plate, but it is safer to know exactly what the piece looks like at the photographic-print stage.

ues: In the lower-left picture the parking
n is backward; bicycle enthusiasts would
bably be quick to point out that some me-
anical features are on the wrong side.

For whatever reason *flopping* a picture—reversing the image—is sometimes
used as a design technique. In the picture at the top nothing seems to
indicate flopping—it would be possible to print either way. In the picture
below are two clues to the flopping—can you spot them? Sometimes very
common details will turn out wrong when a picture is flopped—the position
of buttons on men's and women's clothing, for instance.

An experimental decoration with
starlike forms by the author.

Illustration for a timetable cover for Eastern
Airlines. The illustration is by Paul Williams.

Situations often occur in graphic design in which one subject or a single picture or photograph cannot do justice to the text. This is an opportunity for the designer to resort to *montage*, a technique in which several different elements are combined in a single composition. Photographs or art subjects may be used. The two pieces reproduced here show how related elements can be designed or interwoven to make an interesting and informative whole. The following two pages show how photographic subjects can be used in different ways to develop what must be an interesting spread to people who enjoy football.

The REDSKIN

PRICE 24c
Sales tax 1c
TOTAL 25c
25¢

OPENING GAME · 1949
GRIFFITH STADIUM · WASHINGTON, D.C.

Washington Redskin game program

Turk Edwards, All Pro tackle for
the Boston and Washington
Redskins

Steve Van Buren,
three time NFL
rushing leader for the
Philadelphia Eagle

Sammy Baugh, famed Redskin, is best known as
a passer, but he was equally great kicking the
ball. He still holds most of the NFL punting records
and is the only man ever to lead the league in
punting four straight seasons.

Bill Osmanski was
another in the long line
of great Bear runners. He
scored the first touchdown
in the Bears' 73-0 victory
over the Washington Redskins
in 1940.

Wherever Sammy Baugh went he was besieged by fans for autographs.
The great Redskin quarterback never turned them down.

Bill Dudley, one of
Pittsburgh's greatest
all-around players

Double-page spread from an exciting booklet entitled
Half a Century, reproduced by courtesy of
Kimberly-Clark Corporation, Neenah, Wisconsin.

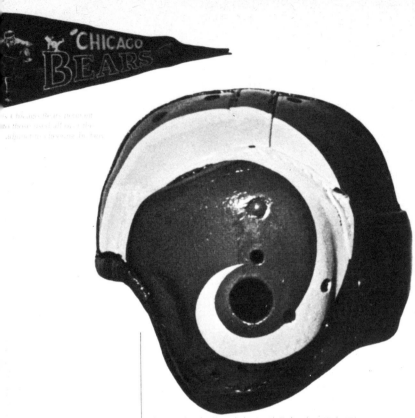

The Chicago Bears pennant was among those used all over today's adjuncts to rooting in pro...

Early Detroit Lion program.

The Los Angeles Rams helmet with its hand-painted ram's horns started the trend to team emblems on headgear. Halfback Fred Gehrke painted it.

Redskin end Charlie Malone is catching a pass during the disastrous 73-0 championship loss to the Bears in 1940.

Jim Conzelman, famous player and later coach of the 1947 champion Chicago Cardinals.

EIN — HIS DAY

s vs. Brooklyn Dodgers

CAPTAIN MEL HEIN
The Giant All-Time Center

NDS   **Sunday, Dec. 1, 1940**

ein gets star treatment on this ants poster. Hein is generally he greatest center in pro history.

Quarterback Sid Luckman and fellow Chicago Bears celebrate their title win over the New York Giants in 1946.

95

ART MECHANICALS

At this point it is hoped that the reader has gathered much information to help him or her become a fine graphic designer and has been inspired to look thoroughly for subjects that will excite even more interest and add to design abilities. To make a rather obvious comparison, it is probable that a good chef spends a great deal of time in the kitchen dealing with minute details. Unless this is so, it is safe to say that the results will never be really distinguished. It is equally true that a good designer is concerned with the smallest details, including the final art mechanicals that go to the printer.

The following pages deal with this important phase of the designer's work. It can be challenging, it is often detailed and tedious, but it should never be boring because it is the final test of a project well done. Since artwork, art mechanicals, or art originals—whatever you call them—are the last step in preparing a job for printing, it is appropriate that the last section of this book deals with this subject. The mechanicals shown here are very, very simple in order to explain what is required clearly. The reader should appreciate the fact that some mechanicals are extremely simple and others are extremely complicated and involved. It should be pointed out— and this is a good place to do so—that some designers specialize in preparing mechanical art, and their services are often utilized in pressing or involved circumstances.

A word of advice: *never* fail to ask the printer for information and instructions about preparing art mechanicals. Printers are often annoyed that they are not asked about this work in advance and rightfully insist that in many instances they should be consulted.

The first important step in preparing mechanicals is to procure efficient equipment. Some of the materials already in use in an artist's studio may be used, but they should be thoroughly checked and put in order. For instance, an inferior T-square that has been dropped or nicked is worthless; a cheap high-school ruling pen should be thrown away. Use the list of tools on the following page as a guide in planning an efficient work area.

Tools and Equipment

Drawing board, drawing table, or drafting table

Steel T-squares—24" and 30"

Ruler—metal edge with inch and pica measurements

Angles—45°-45°-90° and 30°-60°-90°

Circle, oval, and curve guides

Drawing pencils—HB, 2H, and others as desired

Nonreproducing-blue pencils

Erasers

Mechanical drawing instruments—ruling pen, compass, and calipers

Brushes—#2, #5, and #7

Masking tape

Scotch tape

Tracing paper—preferably in pads

Illustration, mounting, and bristol boards (domestic bristol is often adequate and less expensive)

Black and red inks

Fixative

Proportion guide

Screen-tint finder

Rubber cement and rubber-cement thinner

Cutting and single-edge razor blades

Type-specimen books

Colored-paper sample books

Ink-color sample book

Rubylith and/or Amberlith sheets

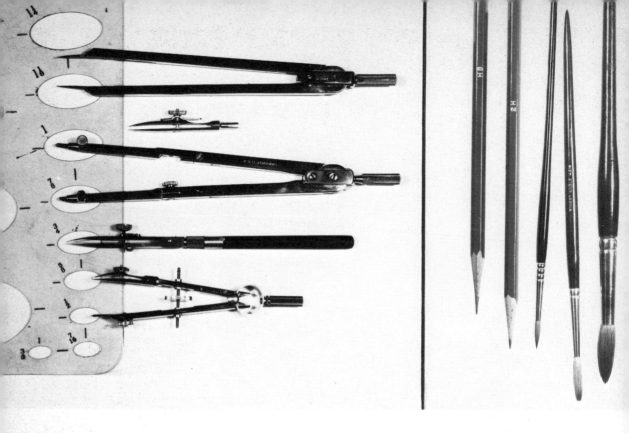

The equipment and tools shown on these two pages are taken from the list on page 97. Of primary importance are the T-square, ruler, and angle pictured opposite and the instruments, pencils, brushes, fixing sprays, and rubber cement shown on this page. The one tool that is not on the list is the airbrush shown below.

The reader is again reminded that good tools are a good investment. Once purchased, instruments must be kept clean and in good condition. Thoughtful use is requisite—for example, nothing ruins a fine brush as quickly as india ink. If possible, have a special brush for this medium and clean it immediately in clear water after use.

The airbrush shown at the right may be completely unknown to many art students since it is often considered too "commercial." However, in the hands of a specialist it is a truly remarkable piece of equipment—and a delicate one. There are many situations in which a bit of retouching is essential to eliminate unwanted details, to accentuate a detail, or to soften a background. Some artists who specialize in production art become very expert in the use of an airbrush, and many graphic artists turn to them for their services.

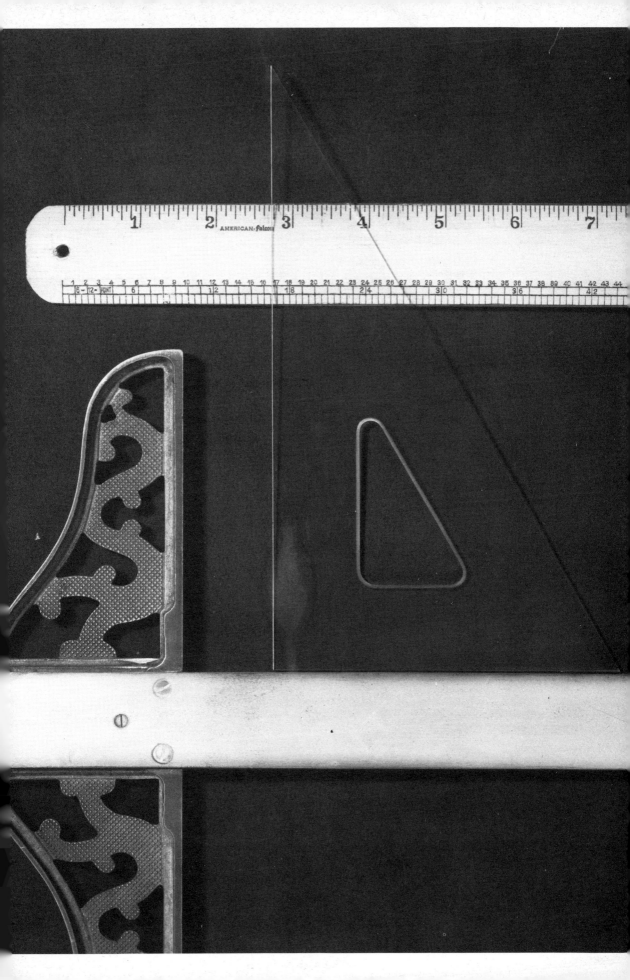

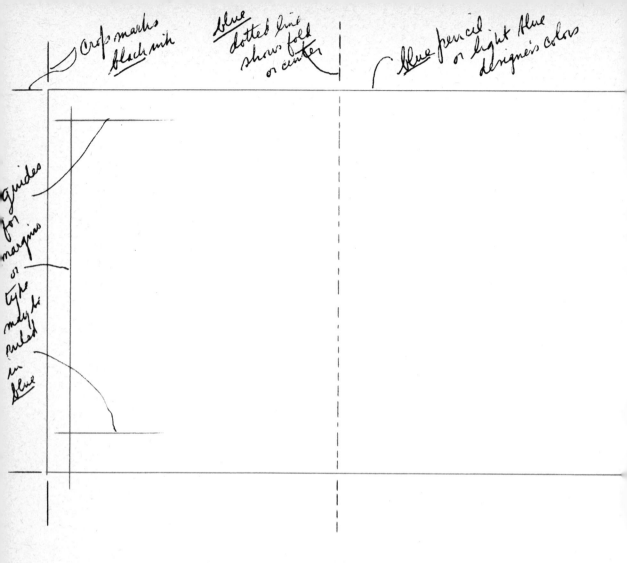

Crop marks black ink

blue dotted line shows fold or center

Blue pencil or light blue designer's colors

Guides for margins or type may be ruled in blue

The next step in preparing finished art mechanicals is to select the surface on which to do them. This can be illustration board, good mounting board, or good bristol board. The mounting board is probably best for general use. If detailed artwork is to be done directly on the board, an illustration or mounting board with the proper surface must be chosen. The best boards for clean linework have hot-press (smooth) surfaces. For washes or tonework a cold-press (mat) surface is best.

Cut a piece of board sufficiently large to leave a 2″ margin around all sides of the piece. It is usually best to do finished art the same size (SS) as the reproduction is to be. In the diagrams on these pages a mechanical for a two-page spread, each page of which is 8½″ × 11″, is being prepared. (The diagrams are shown in reduced size.) The actual size of the board should be 21″ × 15″ (8½″ + 8½″ + 2″ at left + 2″ at right = 21″; 11″ + 2″ at top + 2″ at bottom = 15″).

The next step is to position the illustration or mounting board on the drawing board or table. Align the bottom edge accurately with the blade of the T-square and use short strips of masking tape to secure it in position. With a nonreproducing-blue pencil (it does not photograph on the negatives) mark the dimensions of the pages and draw in the lines. Make a dotted vertical line in blue for the centerfold. None of these lines will show in the reproduction; any lines that *are* to print must be drawn in black or red.

Put in the crop or fold marks. They must be outside of the pages, and, although they are not to print, they should be in black so that the page edges and folds are indicated on the negative. It is a good idea to plot out a plan for the pages. The diagram above should help.

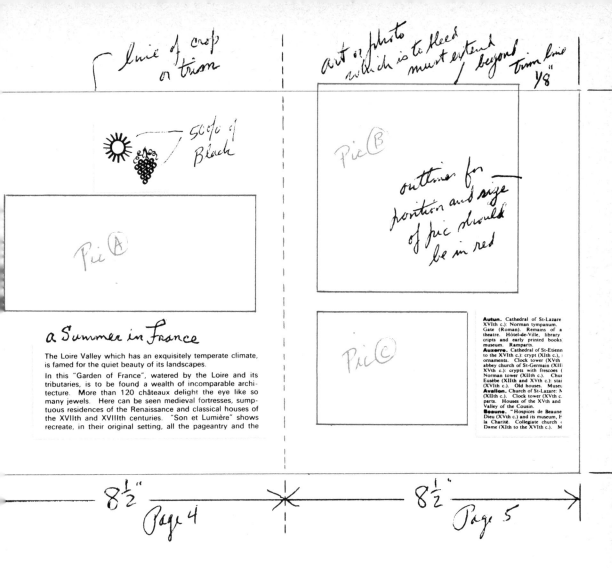

The diagram on this page shows (in miniature) exactly how a piece of finished mechanical art ready to go to the printer should look. The red lines do not print—they are guides only for the position of the photographs—the printer will eliminate them. Reproduction proofs of the text are positioned exactly as they are to print, as are the two pieces of art, the sun and the grapes. The headline, handwritten to give a feeling of informality, was done on a separate piece of thin board and pasted in position. Note that the printer is instructed to screen the two pieces of art to 50% of black: they will look gray in the final reproduction. Instructions are written in blue pencil.

The top picture on the right page is marked to *bleed*. This means that the top edge of the picture is to be printed beyond the edge of the page—this can be done on any of the four sides of a printed sheet but not, of course, at the gutter or fold. The bleed beyond the trim is indicated with a red line, as shown in the reproduction above. To make sure that a picture will not trim short and leave an unwanted white edge instead of a bleed, the bleed allowance should always be ⅛″ or more.

If the pictures on these pages were two- or four-color, their positions and sizes would be indicated in the same way—by a red line. Pictures not on the mechanical should be keyed by letters (A) or numbers (1) in consecutive order, and the keys should be repeated on the mechanical in blue pencil. This is particularly important for a project of many pages.

Sizing photographs was explained on page 89, and the sizing for the layout on the following page was done in the same way as for an actual project. It is important that the sizing of artwork and photography be extremely accurate, for the printer assumes that it is correct and reshooting incorrectly sized negatives is costly.

Pic B 5 5/8 "

3 1/4"

7" pic A

Pic C

The three photographs used in this layout pre
shown as if they were mounted and sized and
the printer. Photographic prints can be mounted
ber cement, by the wax process, or by dry mountin
graphs by the author.

a Summer in France

The Loire Valley which has an exquisitely temperate climate, is famed for the quiet beauty of its landscapes.

In this "Garden of France", watered by the Loire and its tributaries, is to be found a wealth of incomparable architecture. More than 120 châteaux delight the eye like so many jewels. Here can be seen medieval fortresses, sumptuous residences of the Renaissance and classical houses of the XVIIth and XVIIIth centuries. "Son et Lumière" shows recreate, in their original setting, all the pageantry and the

Autun. Cathedral of St-Lazare XVIth c.): Norman tympanum. Gate (Roman). Remains of a theatre. Hôtel-de-Ville, library crypts and early printed books museum. Ramparts.
Auxerre. Cathedral of St-Etienn to the XVth c.): crypt (XIth c.), ornaments. Clock tower (XVth abbey church of St-Germain (XII XVth c.): crypts with frescoes Norman tower (XIIth c.). Chu Eusèbe (XIIth and XVth c.): sta (XVIth c.). Old houses. Muse
Avallon. Church of St-Lazare: N (XIIth c.). Clock tower (XVth c parts. Houses of the XVth and Valley of the Cousin.
Beaune. "Hospices de Beaune Dieu (XVth c.) and its museum, F la Charité. Collegiate church Dame (XIth to the XVIth c.). M

On this page is shown the final printed piece. Remember that for demonstration purposes this is a miniature reproduction of an 8½"-×-11" double-page spread. However, if the spread was to be the same size as the miniature, the procedures would be the same. Note that the largest photograph at the top right bleeds off the top of the page—it was trimmed according to the positioning instructions on the layout. In making a brochure, catalog, or book the pages are not trimmed individually but are bound up and trimmed as a group.

Color artwork, prints, and transparencies must be sized in a similar manner to black-and-white artwork and photography. Color prints may be mounted in the same way as black-and-white prints, as shown on page 102.

Color transparencies are generally protected in acetate envelopes; 35mm transparencies may be mounted in window mounts, as shown below. The cropping and sizing may be done right on the mount.

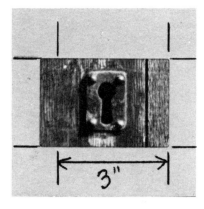

It is sometimes more feasible to mount transparencies in black cards with see-through windows and to mark cropping and sizing in white on the black mat. The pictures on the right, shown in two-color, represent a color transparency for demonstration purposes.

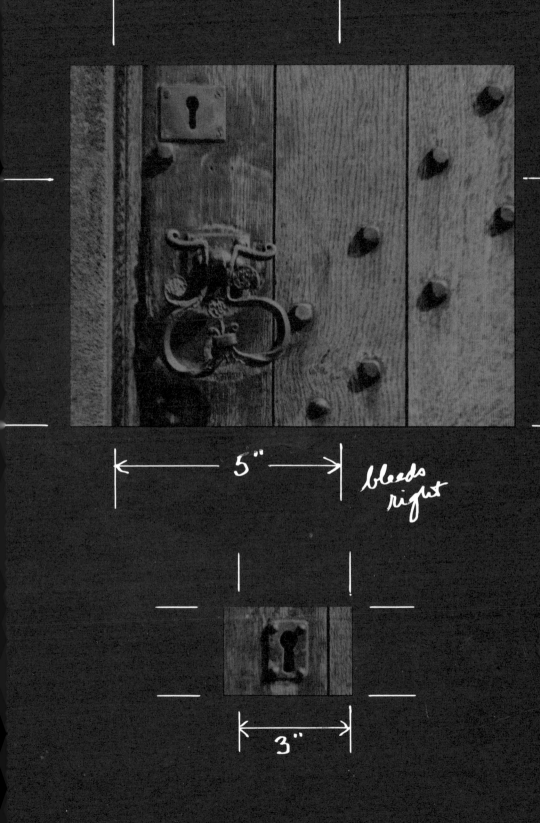

5"

bleeds
right

3"

Progressive Stages from Concept to Finished Project

1. *Preliminary text written.* Following a discussion of the objectives of the project a rough draft of the message(s) is written.
2. *Rough layouts prepared.* The designer makes rough, sketchy layouts to visualize the project and to begin to relate text and design.
3. *Finished text written and approved.* The editor or copywriter, after evaluating criticisms of and suggestions for the rough text, prepares the final text.
4. *Comprehensive layouts developed.* Executives or clients understand the project better if they see finished-looking preliminary designs (*comps*).
5. *Type set in galley form.* Following specification of type (specs) by the designer, galley proofs of the text are prepared. Corrections or additions to the text are made at this point.
6. *Corrections or approvals of galleys.* Corrections or approvals of galleys are returned to the typographer, who then prepares clean, perfect reproduction proofs (repros).
7. *Reproduction proofs.* As the name implies, reproduction proofs are used to reproduce from and are pasted in position on the finished art mechanicals.
8. *Artwork or photography assigned.* The preparation of artwork or photography usually begins as soon as the project is approved. It is usually prepared in a convenient size for the artist or photographer.
9. *Artwork or photography approved.* Artwork or photography, of course, needs to be reviewed and approved by all people involved in the project. Changes or corrections are made at this point.
10. *Art mechanicals developed.* When type repros and art or photography are complete, the final art mechanicals are made.
11. *Artwork or photography sized and cropped.* Since original artwork or photography may be in different dimensions than desired for the finished piece, it must be marked for sizing and cropping.
12. *Art mechanicals approved.* When mechanicals are completed, they must get final approval, which may be the time to make correct estimates for printing.
13. *Art mechanicals to printer.* The printer enters the project and begins to work from the mechanicals. The designer usually goes over the mechanicals carefully with the printer.
14. *Paper selection.* Since paper is a very important part of the project's look and success, the client and the designer may want to select the stock along with the printer.
15. *Brown-line or blue-line proofs.* The printer supplies brown-line or blue-line proofs of the project so that everyone involved may have a last opportunity to check all details.
16. *Printing begins.* Following approval of brown lines or blue lines the actual printing begins. This involves many technical operations.
17. *Proofs from the printer.* On many projects the designer simply specifies paper stock and ink color(s). For important jobs, however, and especially for four-color work the printer furnishes color proofs. These must be carefully reviewed in relation to the originals and corrections made if required. Occasionally a designer may need to check color while a job is on press.
18. *Trimming and binding.* After final printing of the job, which may be in hundreds or thousands of copies, it is bound, trimmed, and ready for delivery.

GLOSSARY

A miniature dictionary of terms used in the graphic arts.

ACETATE transparent material used in preparing separations for finished artwork.

AIRBRUSH the technique of applying paint or dye with an instrument that blows the pigments by air under pressure—used to emphasize or remove details in photography or artwork.

ALTERATION a change made by a client after type has been set. If the typesetter is not at fault, additional charges are legitimate.

AMPERSAND the name for the character "&."

ASCENDER that part of a lowercase letter that extends above the body of the character.

AUTHOR'S ALTERATION (AA) a correcton made by an author, editor, or client on typeset material. They are billed to the author or customer.

BASIS WEIGHT a term used to classify papers denoting the actual weight in pounds of 500 sheets of 25"-×-38" paper.

BENDAY the application of dots, lines, or other textures to a line plate before etching to produce various tonal and textural effects.

BINDING the method by which papers are held together in a printed piece—stapling, sewing, gluing, etc.

BLEED printed material that extends to any edge of a page.

BLOWUP an enlargement from original size.

BODY TYPE type used for large amounts of printed material, such as the text of an advertisement, book, or magazine page.

BOLDFACE heavy, dark type used for emphasis in heads and indexes.

BROCHURE a bound and stitched booklet.

BULLET(S) a dot or series of dots.

CAPS abbreviation for "capitals"; the large letters of an alphabet (uppercase) as opposed to the small letters (lowercase).

CAPTION descriptive text for an illustration, placed adjacently to it.

CARBRO a process of printing full-color photographs.

CAST OFF to estimate the amount of space required for a given amount of text or copy in a given type size.

CENTER SPREAD the two center pages of a booklet or magazine.

CHARACTER a single printed or typewritten letter.

CHARACTER COUNT a method of estimating type sizes and space by counting the number of characters in the text or copy.

COLD TYPE typesetting done by a typewriterlike machine in which a matrix and heat are not used.

COLLAGE a method of creating a piece of art or a design in which various associated or disassociated materials are pasted together on a flat surface.

COLLATE to place pages or forms in proper order or sequence.

COMBINATION PLATE a plate with both line and halftone art.

COMPOSITION typeset material.

CONDENSED TYPE a typeface with narrow characters and vertical design.

CONTACT PRINT a photographic print that is exactly the same size as the negative, made with the film negative and sensitized paper.

CONTINUOUS TONE gradation of tone without halftone dots, as a photograph.

COPY (a) text for an advertisement, magazine, or book. (b) an engraver's term for original artwork.

COPYFITTING any of several methods for estimating the space needed for a given amount of text in a given type size.

COVER the exterior pages of a magazine, catalog, book, referred to as cover 1, cover 2, cover 3, and cover 4: cover 1 indicates the name and sometimes the contents; covers 2, 3, and 4 may contain additional information or advertising.

CROP MARKS indications of where artwork is to be cut or where a bleed page will be cut.

DEADLINE the time set for the delivery of work.

DECKLE EDGE an edge of paper purposely left untrimmed.

DESCENDER the part of a lowercase letter that extends below the body of the character.

DIE-CUTTING the mechanical process of cutting planned shapes in paper, such as a cover in which a circle is cut so that the first page shows through.

DIRECT MAIL material designed and prepared for mail distribution.

DISPLAY (a) a very large type size used for headings. (b) a design generally prepared for dimensional form. (c) the art of show-window design and installation.

DOUBLE SPREAD a design that spreads across two pages.

DRY BRUSH an art technique in which the brush is used with moist—not wet—pigments.

DRY MOUNT a method of mounting photographs and artwork by means of a specially prepared tissue and heated instruments.

DUMMY the preparatory facsimile of a booklet, catalog, etc., usually prepared for purposes of approval but useful to typographers, engravers, and printers in carrying out the requirements of the designer.

DUOTONE the use of a second plate, most often with a second color of ink, to add color or subtlety to a halftone reproduction.

ELECTROTYPE a duplicate engraving plate made from the original.
EM the square of a type body named after the fact that the letter M is often cast on a square body.
EMBOSSING printing a design in relief with dies.
EN half the width of an em.
ENGRAVING a printing plate made by an etching process.
ENLARGEMENT a photographic print that is bigger than the negative.
EXTENDED TYPE a typeface that is wide in character and horizontal in design.

FINISH completed artwork.
FLAP protecting paper placed over the surface of finished art, folded over the top, and pasted to the back.
FOLIO a page number—right-hand pages are always odd; left-hand pages, even.
FONT an assortment of type in one size and style.
FORMAT the general appearance or plan of a printed page.
FOUR-COLOR the exact name for the common term "full-color," denoting the number of plates used in most full-color printing.
FREELANCE an independent artist or designer who does work for different organizations.
FULL-COLOR see four-color.

GALLEY PROOF proofs of type matter not yet in page form.
GLOSSY a photograph or photostat with a very shiny surface.
GRAVURE a printing method that utilizes etched intaglio plates.
GUTTER the center of two pages in a book or magazine.

HALFTONE (a) a printing plate made by photographing the original through a halftone screen. (b) the printed impression from this plate.
HEADING the title on a page, as distinguished from the text material, usually set in larger and/or heavier type.
HOUSE ORGAN a publication or magazine prepared by a company as opposed to a magazine produced for sale.

IMPOSITION the arrangement of plates in proper order for printing.
INITIAL LETTER a larger letter in the first word of text.
INSERT a page or signature printed separately, often on different paper or utilizing different printing methods.
INTERTYPE the trade name for a machine that sets individual type characters (slugs) in a line.

JACKET originally the dustcover for a book, now utilized as a design area for advertising the book.
JUSTIFY typesetting in which all lines are equally wide, often specified as flush left and flush right.

KEY the identification of positions of copy or art in a dummy or comp with letters or other symbols.
KEY DRAWING a master drawing according to which other drawings in separation art are drawn for correct registration; usually the drawing for black.
KEY PLATE the plate according to which other plates are positioned; usually the most detailed plate.

LAYOUT the composition of the elements on a printed page.
LEADER a dot and/or dash in typographic design, often used in statements and reports.
LEADING space between lines of type achieved by inserting thin lead strips of a specified size in points.
LETTERPRESS a printing method in which a raised surface such as type or photoengraving is used.
LETTERSPACING the allowance of more space between letters in typesetting than normal.
LINE artwork with no tonal variations, used to make linecuts. Line art in pencil or chalk usually requires a halftone screen.
LINOTYPE trade name for a machine that sets individual type characters (slugs) in a line.
LOGOTYPE a designed signature or trademark used by a company in advertising—often called a logo.
LOWERCASE the small letters of the alphabet (as opposed to uppercase, the capital letters).
LUDLOW trade name for a process of casting slugs from handset type.

MAKEREADY preparation of a press for printing—putting the type form on the press and evening the impression.
MAKEUP the arrangement of copy and artwork into page form.
MARGIN the space surrounding printed matter on a page.
MAT (a) a window cut from mat or illustration board to protect and enhance a piece of artwork. (b) a papier-mâché matrix in which type is cast.
MATRIX a mold for casting typefaces in monotype and linotype machines.
MEASURE the length of a line of type in picas.
MECHANICAL(S) finished artwork ready for production.
MONOTYPE trade name for a machine that automatically casts and assembles individual letters into lines.
MONTAGE a term applied to a photographic composition in which different elements are superimposed or juxtaposed with each other.

NEGATIVE (a) in photography the image of an original on film or glass from which a print or positive is taken. (b) in a photostat the image of an original on paper from which a print or positive is taken.

OFFSET a printing method in which material is reproduced photographically onto a metal plate.

OPAQUE (a) a nontransparent paint or paper. (b) in photoengraving the painting out of areas on the negative that are not desired on the printing plate.

OVERLAY any material on which artwork is done and which is transparent enough to show other related art. Drawings for secondary colors are often done on overlays, usually acetate.

PAPER material made from straw, rags, fibers, etc., and usually produced in sheets.

PASTE-UP the term applied to the assembly of artwork for printing, including photographs, headings, logos, etc.

PHOTOCOMPOSITION type set by machine onto photographic paper as opposed to metal type on paper proofs.

PHOTOSTAT a photographic method of duplicating originals.

PICA a typographic measurement—about 1/6 of an inch.

PLATE the unit, developed from material prepared by designers and processors, from which the printed impression is made.

POINT a unit of measurement denoting the height of a slug on which a type letter is cast—1 point (pt.) is 1/72 of an inch, or 1/12 of a pica.

POSITIVE an image achieved from a photographic negative corresponding in detail to the original.

PRESS PROOF a proof in one or more colors taken after press makeready.

PRIMARY COLORS red, yellow, and blue printing inks, often called process colors.

PRINTER'S ERROR (PE) a mistake made by a typesetter or printer for which he is responsible and for which the customer is not charged.

PROCESS PLATES the color plates used to print two or more colors; in four-color printing, yellow, red, blue, and black.

PROGRESSIVE PROOFS sets of proofs showing individual colors and combination of colors in process printing. The plates are proved in proper color rotation using inks and paper specified by the printer.

PROOF printed material furnished by typographers or printers for review, corrections, and/or approval. They may be anything from type galleys to proofs of four-color work.

REGISTER the positioning of reproduction plates for printing.

REPRODUCTION PROOFS final proofs of typographic material ready for reproduction.

ROTOGRAVURE a photographic method of gravure printing.

ROUGH a sketch or crude layout.

RUNAROUND type set to fit around an illustration instead of following a column measure.

RUNNING HEAD a title repeated on several consecutive pages.

SANS SERIF a letter or typeface without serifs (see below).

SCREEN the number of dots per square inch in a halftone reproduction.

SEPARATION a plate of one of the colors used to print color artwork.

SERIF a chisellike ending on the stroke of a letter.

SIGNATURE a section of pages in a book—8, 12, 16, or more—folded from a single sheet.

SILKSCREEN a reproduction method in which ink is transferred to the paper through stretched silk.

SMALL CAPS small capital letters used with many roman typefaces for subheads, etc.

SPLIT FOUNTAIN a method of obtaining several colors in one impression by separating inks in the press.

STAT a short term for photostat.

STEREOTYPE a duplicate of a printing plate: a matrix of the original plate is made in papier-mâché, and a cast is taken from it.

TEXT the type on a printed page that carries the story or message. In advertising it is often called copy.

THREE-COLOR PROCESS the reproduction of a full-color original with three colors instead of four. Yellow, red, and blue are usually used.

TINT BLOCK a solid plate used in printing flat colors.

TIP-IN a printed piece that is not bound into a project but inserted separately.

TISSUE a type of paper used in layout work.

TRANSPARENCY a transparent black-and-white or color positive.

TRANSPARENT pigment as opposed to opaque paint or paper.

TRIM the place at which a printed page is cut.

TYPOGRAPHY the setting of metal or photographic letterforms (type).

UPPERCASE the large letters of the alphabet (as opposed to lowercase, the small letters).

VIGNETTE an indistinct or soft edge in a drawing, painting, photograph, or halftone.

WASH a drawing done in a wet medium as opposed to a line drawing.

WATERMARK a design or trademark made into paper during manufacture.

WIDOW a short line at the end of a paragraph of text, often a single word. Many writers will edit the preceding text to eliminate it.

WORK-AND-TURN the printing of both sides of a sheet consecutively. Many modern printing presses print both sides of a sheet simultaneously.

WRAPAROUND the term applied to a printed piece that wraps around other printed material, such as a label.

WRONG FONT a letter that is the wrong typeface or size.

BIBLIOGRAPHY

The publications listed here offer useful information on reproduction in the graphic arts. The reader should be aware that some books on the subject are dull in presentation but contain much of technical value. Others are visually exciting as well as informative.

Ballinger, Raymond A., *Layout and Graphic Design*, Van Nostrand Reinhold Company, New York.
————, *Lettering Art in Modern Use*, Van Nostrand Reinhold Company, New York.
———— and Louise, *Sign, Symbol, and Form*, Van Nostrand Reinhold Company, New York.
Brunner, Felix, *A Handbook of Graphic Reproduction Processes*, Arthur Niggli, Ltd., Teufen AR, Switzerland.
Cooke, Donald E., *Color by Overprinting*, John C. Winston Company, Philadelphia and Toronto.
Craig, James, *Designing with Type*, Watson-Guptill Publications, New York.
————, *Production for the Graphic Designer*, Watson-Guptill Publications, New York.
Curwen, Harold, *Processes of Graphic Reproduction in Printing*, Faber and Faber, Ltd., London.
Eckstein, Arthur and Bernard Stone, *Preparing Art for Printing*, Van Nostrand Reinhold Company, New York.
Hoffmann, Armin, *Graphic Design Manual*, Van Nostrand Reinhold Company, New York.
Hurlburt, Allen, *Publication Design*, Van Nostrand Reinhold Company, New York.
Library of Congress, *Papermaking*, Washington, D.C.
van Uchelen, Rod, *Paste-up,* Van Nostrand Reinhold Company, New York.

In addition to the publications listed above the reader should be aware of material produced by various manufacturers of graphic-arts supplies. Noteworthy are the distinguished publications prepared by paper, type, and transfer-type manufacturers. It may require some initiative to procure this material, but information can be obtained from typesetting houses and wholesale paper distributors in your locality.